Annuals *for* Ontario

Alison Beck
Kathy Renwald

Principal photography by Tim Matheson

© 2001 by Lone Pine Publishing
First printed in 2001   10 9 8 7 6 5 4 3 2 1
Printed in Canada

The Publisher: Lone Pine Publishing

10145 – 81 Avenue	1901 Raymond Ave. SW,
Edmonton, AB T6E 1W9	Suite C, Renton, WA 98055
Canada	USA

Website: http://www.lonepinepublishing.com

Canadian Cataloguing in Publication Data
Beck, Alison, 1971–
  Annuals for Ontario

Includes index.
ISBN 1-55105-247-4

1. Annuals (Plants)—Ontario. 2. Gardening—Ontario. I. Renwald, Kathy, 1951– II. Title.
SB422.B4216 2001   635.9'312'09713   C00-911356-8

Editorial Director: Nancy Foulds
Project Editor: Shelagh Kubish
Editorial: Shelagh Kubish, Dawn Loewen
Illustrations Coordinator: Carol Woo
Photo Editor: Don Williamson
Research Assistant: Allison Penko
Production Manager: Jody Reekie
Book Design: Heather Markham
Cover Design: Robert Weidemann
Layout & Production: Elliot Engley, Heather Markham
Image Editing: Elliot Engley

Photography: All photographs by Tim Matheson (with field identification by Dawna Ehman) or Tamara Eder except Peter Thompstone 54a, 54b, 85a, 85b, 122, 123a, 123b, 139b, 167b, 179b, 190, 191a, 191b, 215a, 215b, 247; David McDonald 57b, 103, 124, 209a; Joan de Grey 57a; Horticolor ©2000 Nova-Photo-Graphik/Horticolor™ 84, 98, 99, 102, 125, 133a, 133b, 193a, 209b; Allison Penko 109b, 196b; EuroAmerican 132; Colin Laroque 10, 15b, 45; Elliot Engley 26a, 26b, 27a, 27b, 27c.

Front cover photographs (clockwise from top left) by Tim Matheson, fuchsia, dahlia, begonia, gazania, zinnia
Back cover author photos: Alison Beck by Alan Bibby, Kathy Renwald by Tim Leyes
Bug Illustrations: Ian Sheldon

We acknowledge the financial support of the Government of Canada through the Book Publishing Industry Development Program (BPIDP) for our publishing activities.

Contents

Acknowledgements

W e express our appreciation to all who were involved in this project. Special thanks are extended to the following organizations and individuals: in Hamilton to the Royal Botanical Gardens; in Niagara to the Niagara Parks Commission; in St. Catharines to the Niagara College Horticulture Program; in Newington to Centre Commons Perennials.

Thanks also to Tim Matheson, Dawna Ehman, Peggy Coulter, Robin and Nancy Matheson, Barbara Matheson; in Vancouver to Acadia Community Garden at UBC, Michael Levenson and the Compost Demonstration Garden, Maple Leaf Nurseries, Pension Fund Realty Ltd. at Park and Tilford Gardens, Odessa Bromeley and Southside Perennials, Board of Parks and Recreation, Southland Nursery, Strathcona Community Gardens, UBC Botanical Gardens, Van Dusen Gardens, West Van Florist, Westrend Gardening; in Victoria to Butchart Gardens; in Rosedale to Minter Gardens; in Edmonton to the Devonian Botanical Gardens, the Muttart Conservatory, Ernst Eder, Heather Markham, Leslie Knight, Bill Kozak, Alex and Bonnie Rosato.

Additional thanks to Peter Thompstone for his generous contribution and involvement in preparing this book.

The Flowers at a Glance

Pictorial Guide in Alphabetical Order, by Common Name

African Daisy
p. 46

Ageratum
p. 48

Amaranth
p. 52

Angel's Trumpet
p. 56

Baby's Breath
p. 60

Bells-of-Ireland
p. 70

Bachelor's Buttons
p. 62

Bacopa
p. 64

Begonia
p. 66

Black-Eyed Susan
p. 72

Blanket Flower
p. 78

Blue Marguerite
p. 82

Black-Eyed Susan Vine
p. 76

Blue Lace Flower
p. 80

Browallia
p. 84

Calendula
p. 86

Candytuft
p. 92

Cape Marigold
p. 96

California Poppy
p. 88

Canterbury Bells
p. 94

Chilean Glory Flower
p. 98

China Aster
p. 100

Chinese Forget-Me-Not
p. 102

Coreopsis
p. 114

Chrysanthemum
p. 104

Cockscomb
p. 106

Coleus
p. 110

Cosmos
p. 116

Cup Flower
p. 122

Dahlberg Daisy
p. 126

Creeping Zinnia
p. 120

Cup-and-Saucer Vine
p. 124

Dahlia
p. 128

Diascia
p. 132

Dusty Miller
p. 134

Dwarf Morning Glory
p. 136

Fan Flower
p. 138

Forget-Me-Not
p. 140

Four-O'Clock Flower
p. 142

Fuchsia
p. 144

Gazania
p. 148

Globe Amaranth
p. 154

Godetia
p. 156

Heliotrope
p. 158

Geranium
p. 150

Hollyhock
p. 162

Impatiens
p. 166

Licorice Plant
p. 170

Lobelia
p. 174

Livingstone Daisy
p. 172

Love-in-a-Mist
p. 176

Madagascar Periwinkle
p. 178

Mallow
p. 180

Marigold
p. 184

Mexican Sunflower
p. 188

Million Bells
p. 190

Monkey Flower
p. 192

Morning Glory
p. 194

Nasturtium
p. 198

Nicotiana
p. 202

Painted-Tongue
p. 206

Passion Flower
p. 208

Petunia
p. 210

Phlox
p. 214

Poppy
p. 216

Portulaca
p. 220

Prairie Gentian
p. 224

Rocket Larkspur
p. 226

Salvia
p. 230

Scabiosa
p. 234

Snapdragon
p. 236

Spider Flower
p. 240

Statice
p. 244

Stock
p. 246

Strawflower
p. 248

Sunflower
p. 250

Swan River Daisy
p. 254

Sweet Alyssum
p. 256

Sweet Pea
p. 258

Verbena
p. 260

Viola
p. 262

Zinnia
p. 266

Introduction

*A*nnuals are plants that germinate, mature, bloom, set seed and die in one growing season. Annuals are sometimes referred to as bedding plants because they provide colour and fill in garden beds. Most annuals are started indoors and then transplanted into the garden after the last spring frost, but some can be sown directly in the garden. A sure sign of spring's arrival is the rush of gardeners to local garden centres, greenhouses and farmers' markets to pick out their new annuals.

The climate in Ontario is excellent for growing most annuals. Summer weather offers warm days and nights and, frequently, high humidity. Annuals that love these conditions thrive in the heat, but aren't as likely to be burned out by summer's end as they would be in the southern U.S. where the heat is far greater. The downside to all this warm weather is that many annuals that prefer cool summer weather don't do as well in Ontario and tend to die back over the hottest part of the season. Keeping them well watered and out of the full sun will often encourage them to revive as cooler fall weather sets in. Gardeners in northern Ontario may find they have more success with violas, lobelia and candytuft than do southern gardeners.

In Ontario the last spring frost falls anywhere from April to June and the first fall frost between September and November depending on where in the province you are gardening. Though the season length varies greatly, most gardeners

Mixed annual gardens

in Ontario can expect a frost-free period of at least four or five months which gives annuals plenty of time to mature and fill the garden with abundant colour. Gardeners in southern Ontario have the longest season and may wish to take advantage of warmer springs and falls by making additional plantings in those seasons. Flowers that tend to fade out in excessive heat can be planted in early spring and enjoyed until the summer heat causes them to die back. Make a sowing of these same frost-tolerant plants in August, and they will thrive in the cooler weather of fall.

Rainfall also varies in Ontario. One effect of the Great Lakes is a normally regular rainfall, and with a good mulch to prevent water loss, most plants will usually need very little supplemental watering. In a dry year, however, a month or more may pass with no significant rainfall, and in these years supplemental watering will be necessary.

Annuals are popular because they produce lots of flowers, in a wide variety of colours, over a long period of time. Many annuals bloom continuously from spring right through until early fall. Beyond this basic appeal, gardeners are constantly finding new ways to include annuals in their gardens, using them to accent areas in an established border, featuring them as the main attraction in a new garden, or combining them with trees, shrubs, perennials and even vegetables. Many annuals are adapted to a variety of growing conditions, from hot, dry sun to cool, damp shade. They are fun for beginners and experienced gardeners alike and, because annuals are temporary and inexpensive, they can be easily replaced if they are undesirable or past their prime.

Some of the most popular, easy to grow and reliable annuals include geraniums, petunias, impatiens and marigolds, but the selection of annuals is increasing every year. New species have been introduced from other parts of the world. There are new and sometimes improved varieties of old favourites with an expanded colour range or increased pest resistance. The use of heritage varieties has been revived partly because many gardeners are concerned with over-hybridization and interested in organic gardening.

When new varieties are introduced, some may experience a short period of popularity but are soon forgotten. Greatly improved varieties that have been tried in gardens across the United States and Canada may be judged by members of the horticultural industry to become 'All-American Selections Winners.' These outstanding plants are the most widely known and frequently grown.

AVERAGE LAST FROST DATE

May 24–June 10

May 5–24

April 15–May 5

MOOSONEE

Lake Nipigon

KENORA

HEARST

TIMMINS

THUNDER BAY

Lake of the Woods

Lake Superior

SUDBURY

SAULT STE. MARIE

NORTH BAY

PEMBROKE

OTTAWA

KINGSTON

Lake Huron

TORONTO

Lake Ontario

HAMILTON

Lake Michigan

SARNIA

WINDSOR

Lake Erie

ANNUALS IN THE GARDEN

*T*he short life of annuals allows gardeners a large degree of flexibility and freedom when planning a garden. Where trees and shrubs form the permanent structure or the bones of the garden, and perennials and groundcovers fill the spaces between them, annuals add bold patterns and bright splashes of colour. Include annuals anywhere that you would like some variety and an extra splash of colour—in pots staggered up porch steps or on a deck, in windowsill planters or in hanging baskets. Even well-established gardens are brightened and given a new look with the addition of annual flowers.

Something as simple as a planting of impatiens under a tree can be different each year with different varieties and colour combinations. When planning your garden, consult as many sources as you can. Look through gardening books and ask friends and greenhouse experts for advice. Notice what you like or dislike about various gardens, and make a list of the plants you would like to include in your garden.

You can create whatever style garden you want by cleverly mixing annuals. A tidy, symmetrical, formal garden can be enhanced by adding only a few types of annuals or by choosing annuals of the same flower colour. In the same garden adding many different species and colours of annuals would relax the neat plantings of trees and shrubs. An informal, cottage-style garden can be a riot of plants and colours. The same garden will look less chaotic and even soothing if you use several species that bloom in cool shades of blue and purple.

When choosing annuals most people make the colour, size and shape of the flowers their prime considerations. Other things to consider are the size and shape of the plant and leaves. A variety of flower and plant sizes, shapes and colours will make your garden more interesting. Consult the Quick Reference Chart on p. 270.

Colours have different effects on our senses. Cool colours such as purple, blue and green are soothing and relaxing and can make a small garden appear larger. Some annuals with cool colours are lobelia, ageratum and browallia. Warm colours such as red, orange and yellow are more stimulating and appear to fill larger spaces. Warm colours can make even the largest, most imposing garden seem warm and welcoming. Some annuals with warm colours are salvia, calendula and cockscomb.

If you work long hours and have time to enjoy your garden only in the evenings, you may want to consider pale colours such as white and yellow. These show up well at dusk and even at night. Some plants have flowers that open only in the evenings and often have fragrant blossoms that add an attractive dimension to the evening garden. Moonflower is a twining vine-like plant with large, white, fragrant flowers that open when the sun sets.

Foliage colour varies a great deal as well. Some annuals are grown for their interesting or colourful foliage

Informal border

Formal border

and not for the flowers at all, yet some plants have both interesting foliage and flowers. Leaves can be in any shade of green and may be covered in a soft white down or they can be so dark they appear to be almost black. Some foliage is patterned or has veins that contrast with the colour of the leaves. Foliage plants such as coleus are often used by themselves while others such as dusty miller provide an interesting backdrop against brightly coloured flowers.

Coleus is available in a multitude of colours and leaf patterns.

ANNUALS WITH INTERESTING FOLIAGE
Amaranth 'Illumination'
Begonia
Coleus
Dusty Miller
Licorice Plant
Nasturtium
Sweet Potato Vine

Texture is another element to consider when planning a garden. Both flowers and foliage have a visual texture. Larger leaves appear coarse in texture and can make a garden appear smaller and more shaded. Coarse-textured flowers appear bold and dramatic and can be seen from farther away. Small leaves appear fine in texture, and these create a sense of increased space and light. Fine-textured flowers appear soothing and even a little mysterious. Sometimes the flowers and foliage of a plant have contrasting textures. Using a variety of textures helps make a garden interesting and appealing.

The interesting foliage of Sweet Potato Vine combines well with fine-textured Lobelia (above).

Coarse-textured Teddy Bear Sunflower (below)

FINE-TEXTURED ANNUALS
Bacopa
Dahlberg Daisy
Lobelia
Swan River Daisy
Sweet Alyssum

COARSE-TEXTURED ANNUALS
Dahlia (large flowered)
Chrysanthemum
Sunflower
Sweet Potato Vine
Zinnia

GETTING STARTED

*F*inding the right annuals for your garden requires experimentation and creativity. Before you start planting, consider the growing conditions in your garden; these conditions will influence not only the types of plants you select, but also the location in which you plant them. Plants will be healthier and less susceptible to problems if grown in optimum conditions. It is difficult to significantly modify your garden's existing conditions; an easier approach is to match the plants to the garden.

The levels of light, porosity and pH; the texture of soil; the amount of exposure in your garden; and the plants' tolerance to frost are guidelines for your plant selection. Sketching your garden may help you visualize how various conditions might affect your planting decisions. Note shaded areas, low-lying or wet areas, exposed or windy sections, etc. Understanding your garden's growing conditions will help you learn where plants will perform best and prevent you from making costly mistakes in your planning. Consult the Quick Reference Chart on p. 270.

LIGHT

There are four levels of light in a garden: full sun, partial shade, light shade and full shade. Available light is affected by buildings, trees, fences and the position of the sun at different times of the day and year. Knowing what light is available in your garden will help you determine where to place each plant.

Marigold (above), Forget-me-not (below)

Plant your annuals where they will grow best. For hot and dry areas and for low-lying, damp sections of the garden, select plants that prefer those conditions. Experimenting with annuals will help you learn about the conditions of your garden.

Sun-loving plants may become tall and straggly and flower poorly in too much shade. Shade-loving plants may get scorched leaves or even wilt and die if they get too much sun. Many plants tolerate a wide range of light conditions.

ANNUALS FOR SUN
Amaranth
Cockscomb
Cosmos
Geranium
Heliotrope
Marigold
Portulaca
Spider Flower
Statice

ANNUALS FOR SHADE
Browallia
Busy Lizzie Impatiens
Canterbury Bells
Forget-me-not
Godetia
Nicotiana
Viola

ANNUALS FOR ANY LIGHT
Black-eyed Susan
Coleus
Cup Flower
Fan Flower
Licorice Plant
Lobelia
Nasturtium
New Guinea Impatiens
Wax Begonia

Plants in *full-sun* locations, such as along south-facing walls, receive direct sunlight for all or most of the day. Locations classified as *partial shade*, such as east- or west-facing walls, receive direct sunlight for part of the day and shade for the rest. *Light-shade* locations receive shade for most or all of the day, although some sunlight does filter through to ground level. An example of a light-shade location might be the ground under a small-leaved tree such as a birch. *Full-shade* locations, which would include the north side of a house, receive no direct sunlight.

SOIL

Soil quality is an extremely important element of a healthy garden. Plant roots rely on the air, water and nutrients that are held within soil. Of course, plants also depend on soil to hold them upright. The soil in turn benefits from plant roots breaking down large soil particles. Plants prevent soil erosion by binding together small particles and reducing the amount of exposed surface. When plants die and break down they add organic nutrients to soil and feed beneficial micro-organisms.

Black-eyed Susan

Soil is made up of particles of different sizes. Sand particles are the largest—water drains quickly from sandy soil and nutrients tend to get washed away. Sandy soil does not compact very easily because the large particles leave air pockets between them. Clay particles, which are the smallest, can be seen only through a microscope. Clay holds the most nutrients, but it also compacts easily and has little air space. Clay is slow to absorb water and equally slow to let it drain. Most soils are composed of a combination of different particle sizes and are called loams.

It is important to consider the pH level (the scale on which acidity or alkalinity is measured) of soil, which influences the availability of nutrients. Most plants thrive in soil with a pH between 5.5 and 7.5. Soil pH varies a great deal from place to place in Ontario. Testing kits can be purchased at most garden centres. There are also soil-testing labs that can fully analyze the pH as well as the quantities of various nutrients in your soil. The acidity of soil can be reduced with the addition of horticultural lime or wood ashes. For plants that prefer a pH that varies greatly from that of your garden soil, you might wish to use planters or create raised beds where it is easier to control and alter the pH level of soil.

Water drainage is affected by soil type and terrain in your garden. Plants that prefer well-drained soil and do not require a large amount of moisture grow well on a sloping hillside garden with rocky soil. Water retention in these areas can be improved through the addition of organic matter. Plants that thrive on a consistent water supply or boggy conditions are ideal for low-lying areas that retain water for longer periods or hardly drain at all. In extremely wet areas, you can improve drainage with the addition of sand or gravel or by creating raised beds.

ANNUALS FOR MOIST SOIL

Forget-me-not
Mallow
Viola
Spider Flower (see next page)

Spider Flower (above), Coreopsis (below)

ANNUALS FOR DRY SOIL
Cape Marigold
Coreopsis
Cosmos
Marigold
Portulaca

Exposure

Your garden is exposed to wind, heat, cold and rain, and some plants are better adapted than others to withstand the potential damage of these forces. Buildings, walls, fences, hills, hedges, trees and even tall perennials influence and often reduce exposure.

Wind and heat are the most likely elements to cause damage to annuals. The sun can be very intense, and heat can rise quickly on a sunny afternoon. Plant annuals that tolerate or even thrive in hot weather in the hot spots in your garden.

Too much rain can be damaging to plants, as can over-watering. Early in the season, seeds or seedlings can be washed away in heavy rain. A light mulch will help prevent this problem. Established annuals (or their flowers) can be beaten down by heavy rain. Most annuals will recover, but some, like petunias, are slow to do so. Choose plants or varieties that are quick to recover from rain damage in exposed sites. Many of the small-flowered petunia varieties now available are quick to recover from heavy rain.

Hanging moss-lined baskets are susceptible to wind and heat exposure, losing water from the soil surface and the leaves. Water can evaporate from all sides of a moss basket, and in hot or windy locations moisture can be depleted very quickly. Hanging baskets look wonderful, but watch for wilting and water the baskets regularly to keep them looking great.

Frost Tolerance

When planting annuals, consider their ability to tolerate an unexpected frost. The dates for last frost and first frost vary greatly from region to region in North America. In Ontario, southern gardens may have a last frost in April while gardens in the north may have a last frost in early June. The map on p. 13 gives a general idea of when you can expect your last frost date. Keep in mind that these dates can vary greatly from year to year and within the general regions. Your local garden centre should be able to provide more precise information on frost expectations for your particular area.

Annuals are grouped into three categories based on how tolerant they are of cold weather: they are either hardy, half-hardy or tender. Consult the Quick Reference Chart on p. 270.

Mulch helps retain water and keeps down weeds.

Hardy annuals can tolerate low temperatures and even frost. They can be planted in the garden early and may continue to flower long into fall or even winter. I had hardy calendulas planted close to the house and they continued to flower even after a snowfall covered them. Many hardy annuals are sown directly in the garden before the last frost date.

Half-hardy annuals can tolerate a light frost but will be killed by a heavy one. These annuals can be planted out around the last frost date and will generally benefit from being started early from seed indoors.

The newer petunias, such as Purple Wave, need diligent watering when planted in hanging pots.

Tender annuals have no frost tolerance at all and might suffer even if the temperatures drop to a few degrees above freezing. These plants are often started early indoors and not planted in the garden until the last frost date has passed and the ground has had a chance to warm up. The advantage to these annuals is that they are often tolerant of hot summer temperatures.

Protecting plants from frost is relatively simple. Plants can be covered overnight with sheets, towels, burlap or even cardboard boxes. Refrain from using plastic because it doesn't retain heat and therefore doesn't provide plants with any insulation.

PREPARING THE GARDEN

*T*aking the time to properly prepare your flowerbeds will save you time and effort over the summer. Starting out with as few weeds as possible and with well-prepared soil that has had organic material added will give your annuals a good start. For container gardens, use potting soil because regular garden soil loses its structure when used in pots, quickly compacting into a solid mass that drains poorly.

Loosen the soil with a large garden fork and remove the weeds. Avoid working the soil when it is very wet or very dry because you will damage the soil structure by breaking down the pockets that hold air and water. Add organic matter and work it into the soil with a spade or rototiller.

Organic matter is a small but important component of soil. It increases the water-holding and nutrient-holding capacity of sandy soil and binds together the large particles. In a clay soil, organic matter will increase the water-absorbing and draining potential by opening up spaces between the tiny particles. Common organic additives for your soil include grass clippings, shredded leaves, peat moss, chopped straw, well-rotted manure and composted hemlock bark.

COMPOSTING

Any organic matter you add will be of greater benefit to your soil if it has been composted first. In natural environments, compost is created when leaves, plant bits and other debris are broken down on the soil surface. This process will also take place in your garden beds if you work fresh organic matter into the soil. However, micro-organisms that break organic matter down use the same nutrients as your plants. The tougher the organic matter, the more nutrients in the soil will be used trying to break the matter down. This will rob your plants of vital nutrients, particularly nitrogen. Also, fresh organic matter and garden debris might encourage or introduce pests and diseases in your garden.

It is best to compost organic matter before adding it to your garden beds. A compost pile or bin, which can be built or purchased, creates a controlled environment where organic matter can be fully broken down before being introduced to your garden. Good composting methods also reduce the possibility of spreading pests and diseases.

Creating compost is a simple process. Kitchen scraps, grass clippings and fall leaves will slowly break down if left in a pile. The process can be sped up by following a few simple guidelines.

Your compost pile should contain both dry and fresh materials, with a larger proportion of dry matter such as chopped straw, shredded leaves or sawdust. Fresh green matter, such as vegetable scraps, grass clippings or pulled weeds, breaks down quickly and produces nitrogen, which feeds the decomposer organisms while they break down the tougher dry matter.

Layer the green matter with the dry matter and mix in small amounts of soil from your garden or previously

Compost worms

Wooden compost bins (above), plastic (below)

Composting materials

Such a high temperature will destroy weed seeds and kill many damaging organisms. Most beneficial organisms will not be killed unless the temperature rises higher than this. To monitor the temperature of the compost near the middle of the pile you will need a thermometer that is attached to a long probe, similar to a large meat thermometer. Turn your compost once the temperature drops. Turning and aerating the pile will stimulate the process to heat up again. The pile can be left to sit without turning and will eventually be ready to use if you are willing to wait several months to a year.

Avoid adding diseased or pest-ridden materials to your compost pile. If the damaging organisms are not destroyed they could be spread throughout your garden. If you do add material you suspect of harbouring pests or diseases, add it near the centre of the pile where the temperature is highest.

finished compost. The addition of soil or compost will introduce beneficial micro-organisms. If the pile seems very dry, sprinkle some water between the layers—the compost should be moist but not soaking wet, like a wrung-out sponge. Adding nitrogen, like that found in fertilizer, will speed up decomposition. Avoid strong concentrations that can kill beneficial organisms.

Each week or two, use a pitchfork to turn the pile over or poke holes into it. This will help aerate the material, which will speed up decomposition. A compost pile that is kept aerated can generate a lot of heat. Temperatures can reach up to 71° C (160° F).

When you can no longer recognize the matter that you put into the compost bin, and the temperature no longer rises upon turning, your compost is ready to be mixed into your garden beds. Getting to this point can take as little as one month and will leave you with organic material that is rich in nutrients and beneficial organisms.

Compost can also be purchased from most garden centres. Whether you use your own or store-bought compost, add a trowelful of compost to the planting hole and mix it into the garden soil before adding your annual.

Selecting Annuals

*M*any gardeners consider the trip to the local garden centre to pick out their annual plants an important rite of spring. Other gardeners find it rewarding to start their own annuals from seed. There are benefits to both methods and many gardeners choose to use a combination of the two. Purchasing plants provides you with plants that are well grown and often already in bloom, which is useful if you don't have the room or the facilities to start seeds. Some seeds require specific conditions that are difficult to achieve in a house or they have erratic germination rates, which makes starting them yourself impractical. Starting from seed may offer you a greater selection of species and varieties as seed catalogues often list many more plants than are offered at garden centres. Starting annuals from seed is discussed on p. 27.

Plants at garden centre (above)

Purchased annual plants are grown in a variety of containers. Some are sold in individual pots, some in divided cell-packs and others in undivided trays. Each type has advantages and disadvantages.

Annuals in individual pots are usually well established and have plenty of space for root growth. These annuals have probably been seeded in flat trays and then transplanted into individual pots once they developed a few leaves. The cost of labour, pots and

Lobelia grown in cell packs

soil can make this option more expensive. If you are planting a large area you may also find it difficult to transport large numbers of plants.

Annuals grown in cell-packs are often inexpensive and hold several plants, making them easy to transport. There is less damage to the roots of the plants when they are

Plant ready for potting.

Plant on right is root-bound.

Regardless of the type of container, often the best plants to choose are those not yet flowering. These plants are younger and are unlikely to be root-bound. Check for roots emerging from the holes at the bottom of the cells or gently remove the plant from the container to look at the roots. Too many roots means that the plant is too mature for the container, especially if the roots are wrapped around the inside of the container in a thick web. Such plants are slow to establish once they are transplanted into the garden.

The plants should be compact and have good colour. Healthy leaves look firm and vibrant. Unhealthy leaves may be wilted, chewed or dis-coloured. Tall, leggy plants have likely been deprived of light. Sickly plants may not survive being transplanted and may spread pests or diseases to the rest of your garden.

Once you get your annuals home, water them if they are dry. Annuals growing in small containers may require water more than once a day. Begin to harden off the plants so they can be transplanted into the garden as soon as possible. Your annuals are probably accustomed to growing in the sheltered environment of a greenhouse, and they will need to become accustomed to the climate outdoors. They can be placed out-doors in a lightly shaded spot each day and brought into a sheltered porch, garage or house each night for about a week. This will acclimatize them to your garden.

transplanted, but because each cell is quite small, it doesn't take too long for a plant to become root-bound.

Annuals grown in undivided trays have plenty of room for root growth and can be left in the trays for longer than other types of containers; how-ever, their roots tend to become entangled, making the plants difficult to separate.

STARTING ANNUALS FROM SEED

*T*here are dozens of catalogues from different growers offering a varied selection of annuals that you can start from seed. Many gardeners while away chilly winter evenings by poring through seed catalogues and planning their spring and summer gardens.

Seedlings in tray (above)

Starting your own annuals can save you money, particularly if you need a lot of plants. The basic equipment necessary is not expensive, and most seeds can be started in a sunny window. However, you may encounter a problem of limited space. One or two trays of annuals don't take up too much room, but storing more than that may be unreasonable. This is why many gardeners start a few specialty plants themselves but purchase the bulk of their annuals already started from a garden centre.

Seeding into cell-packs (above)
Nasturtiums repotted into peat pots (below)

Each plant in this book will have specific information on starting it from seed, but there are a few basic steps that can be followed for all seeds. The easiest way for the home gardener to start seeds is in cell-packs in trays with plastic dome covers. The cell-packs keep roots separated, and the tray and dome keep moisture in.

Seeds can also be started in pots, peat pots or peat pellets. The advantage to starting in peat pots or pellets is that you will not disturb the roots when

Direct seed Baby's Breath, Poppies and Rocket Larkspur.

you transplant your annuals. When planting peat pots into the garden, be sure to remove the top couple of inches of pot. If any of the pot is sticking up out of the soil, it can wick moisture away from your plant.

Use a growing mix (soil mix) that is intended for seedlings. These mixes are very fine, usually made from peat moss, vermiculite and perlite. The mix will have good water-holding capacity and will have been sterilized in order to prevent pests and diseases from attacking your tender young seedlings. One problem that can be caused by soil-borne fungi is damping off. The affected seedling will appear to have been pinched at soil level. The pinched area blackens and the seedling topples over and dies. Using sterile soil mix, keeping soil evenly moist and maintaining good air circulation will prevent the problem of damping off.

Fill your pots or seed trays with the soil mix and firm it down slightly. Soil that is too firmly packed will not

drain well. Wet the soil before planting your seeds to prevent them from getting washed around. Large seeds can be planted one or two to a cell, but smaller seeds may have to be placed in a folded piece of paper and sprinkled evenly over the soil surface. Very tiny seeds, like those of begonias, can be mixed with fine sand before being sprinkled evenly across the soil surface.

Small seeds will not need to be covered with any more soil, but medium-sized seeds can be lightly covered, and large seeds can be poked into the soil. Some seeds need to be exposed to light in order to germinate; these should be left on the soil surface regardless of their size.

Place pots or flats of seeds in plastic bags to retain humidity while the seeds are germinating. Many planting trays come with clear plastic covers which can be placed over the trays to keep the moisture in. Remove the plastic once the seeds have germinated.

Water seeds and small seedlings with a fine spray from a hand-held mister—small seeds can easily be washed around if the spray is too strong. I recall working at a greenhouse where the seed trays containing sweet alyssum were once watered a little too vigorously. Sweet alyssum was soon found growing just about everywhere—with other plants, in the gravel on the floor, even in some of the flowerbeds. The lesson is 'water gently.' A less hardy species would not have come up at all if its seeds were washed into an adverse location.

Seeds provide all the energy and nutrients that young seedlings require. Small seedlings will not need to be fertilized until they have about four or five true leaves. When the first leaves that sprouted begin to shrivel, the plant has used up all its seed energy and you can begin to use a fertilizer diluted to a quarter strength when feeding seedlings or young plants.

If the seedlings get too big for their containers before you are ready to plant them out, you may have to pot them to prevent them from becoming root-bound. Harden plants off by exposing them to sunnier, windier conditions and fluctuating outdoor temperatures for increasing periods of time every day for at least a week.

Some seeds can be started directly in the garden. The procedure is similar to that of starting seeds indoors. Start with a well-prepared bed that has been smoothly raked. The small furrows left by the rake will help hold moisture and prevent the seeds from being washed away. Sprinkle the seeds onto the soil and cover them lightly with peat moss or more soil. Larger seeds can be planted slightly deeper into the soil. You may not want to sow very tiny seeds directly in the garden because they can blow or wash away. The soil should be kept moist to ensure even germination. Use a gentle spray to avoid washing the seeds around the bed because they inevitably pool into dense clumps. Covering your newly seeded bed with chicken wire, an old sheet or some thorny branches will discourage pets from digging.

California Poppy

Some annuals are good choices for direct sowing. For example, you can direct sow annuals with large or quick-germinating seeds or annuals that are difficult to transplant.

ANNUALS FOR DIRECT SEEDING
Amaranth
Baby's Breath
Bachelor's Buttons
Black-eyed Susan
Calendula
California Poppy
Candytuft
Chrysanthemum
Cockscomb
Cosmos
Forget-me-not
Godetia
Mallow
Nasturtium
Phlox
Poppy
Rocket Larkspur
Spider Flower
Sunflower
Sweet Pea
Zinnia

GROWING ANNUALS

Once your annuals are hardened off it is time to plant them out. If your beds are already prepared you are ready to start. The only tool you are likely to need is a trowel. Be sure you have set aside enough time to do the job. You don't want to have young plants out of their pots and not finish planting them. If they are left out in the sun they can quickly dry out and die. To help avoid this problem choose an overcast day for planting out.

PLANTING

Moisten the soil to aid the removal of the plants from their containers. Push on the bottom of the cell or pot with your thumb to ease the plants out. If the plants were growing in an undivided tray then you will have to gently untangle the roots. If the roots are very tangled, immerse them in water and wash some of the soil away. This should free the plants from one another. If you must handle the plant, hold it by a leaf to avoid crushing the stems. Remove and discard any damaged leaves or growth.

The rootball should contain a network of white plant roots. If the rootball is densely matted and twisted, break it apart in order to encourage the roots to extend and grow outward. Do so by breaking apart the tangles a bit with your thumbs. New root growth will start from the breaks allowing the plant to spread outwards.

Insert your trowel into the soil and pull it towards you creating a wedge. Place your annual into the hole and firm the soil around the plant with your hands. Water newly planted annuals gently but thoroughly. Until they are established they will need regular watering for a few weeks.

You don't have to be conservative when arranging your flowerbeds. Though formal bedding-out patterns are still used in many parks and gardens, plantings can be made in casual groups and natural drifts. The quickest way to space out your annuals is to remove them from their containers and randomly place them onto the bed. This will allow you to mix colours and plants without too much planning. Plant a small section at a time—don't allow the roots to dry out. This is especially important if you have a large bed to plant.

If you are just adding a few annuals here and there to accent your shrub and perennial plantings, plant in groups. Random clusters of three to five plants add colour and interest.

Combine the low-growing or spreading annuals with tall or bushy ones. Keep the tallest plants towards the back and smallest plants towards the front of the bed. This improves the visibility of the plants and hides the often unattractive lower limbs of taller plants. Be sure to leave your plants enough room to spread. They may look lonely and far apart when you first plant them, but annuals will quickly grow to fill in the space.

Some annuals require more care than others do, but most require minimal care once established. Weeding, watering and deadheading are a few of the basic tasks that will keep your garden looking its best.

WEEDING

Controlling weed populations keeps the garden healthy and neat. Weeding may not be anyone's favourite task, but it is essential. Weeds compete with your plants for light, nutrients and space, and they can also harbour pests and diseases.

Weeds can be pulled by hand or with a hoe. Shortly after a rainfall, when the soil is soft and damp, is the easiest time to pull weeds. A hoe scuffed quickly across the soil surface will uproot small weeds and sever larger ones from their roots. Try to pull weeds out while they are still small. Once they are large enough to flower, many will quickly set seed; then you will have an entire new generation to worry about.

MULCHING

A layer of mulch around your plants will prevent weeds from germinating by preventing sufficient light from reaching the seeds. Those that do germinate will be smothered or will find it difficult to get to the soil surface,

Even with minimal care Mallow looks bright.

WATERING

Water thoroughly but infrequently. Annuals given a light sprinkle of water every day will develop roots that stay close to the soil surface, making the plants vulnerable to heat and dry spells. Annuals given a deep watering once a week will develop a deeper root system. In a dry spell they will be adapted to seeking out the water trapped deeper in the ground. Use mulch to prevent water from evaporating out of the soil.

Be sure the water penetrates at least 10 cm (4") into the soil. To save time, money and water you may wish to install an irrigation system. Irrigation systems apply the water exactly where it is needed, near the roots, and reduce the amount of water lost to evaporation. They can be very complex or very simple depending on your needs. A simple irrigation system would involve laying soaker hoses around your garden beds under the mulch. Consult with your local garden centres or landscape professionals for more information. Annuals in hanging baskets and planters will probably need to be watered more frequently than plants in the ground. The smaller the container the more often the plants will need watering. Containers and hanging moss baskets may need to be watered twice daily during hot, sunny weather.

exhausting their energy before getting a chance to grow.

Mulch also helps maintain consistent soil temperatures and ensures that moisture is retained more effectively. In areas that receive heavy wind or rainfall, mulch can protect soil and prevent erosion. Mulching is effective in garden beds and planters.

Organic mulches include materials such as compost, bark chips, grass clippings or shredded leaves. These mulches add nutrients to soil as they break down, thus improving the quality of the soil and ultimately the health of your plants.

Spread about 5 cm (2–3") of mulch over the soil after you have planted your annuals. Don't pile the mulch too thick around the crowns and stems of your annuals. Mulch that is too close up against plants traps moisture, prevents air circulation and encourages fungal disease. As your mulch breaks down over summer, be sure to replenish it.

FERTILIZING

Your local garden centre should carry a good supply of both organic and chemical fertilizers. Follow the directions carefully because using too much fertilizer can kill your plants by burning their roots. Whenever possible, use organic fertilizers because they are generally less concentrated and less likely to burn your plants.

Many annuals will flower most profusely if they are fertilized regularly. Some gardeners fertilize hanging baskets and container gardens every time they water—use a very dilute fertilizer so as not to burn the plants. However, too much fertilizer can result in plants that produce weak growth that is susceptible to pest and disease problems. Some plants, like nasturtiums, grow better without fertilizer and may produce few or no flowers when fertilized excessively.

Fertilizer comes in many forms. Liquids or water-soluble powders are easiest to use when watering. Slow-release pellets or granules are mixed into the garden or potting soil or sprinkled around the plant and left to work over summer.

Impatiens never need deadheading.

GROOMING

Good grooming will keep your annuals healthy and neat, make them flower more profusely and help prevent pest and disease problems. Grooming may include pinching, deadheading, trimming and staking.

Pinch out any straggly growth and the tips of leggy annuals. Plants in cell-packs may have developed straggly growth trying to get light. Pinch back the long growth when planting to encourage bushier growth.

Deadheading flowers is important in maintaining the health of annuals. Get into the habit of picking off spent flowers as you are looking around your garden to save yourself a big job later. Some plants, such as impatiens and wax begonias, are self-cleaning, meaning that they drop their faded blossoms on their own.

If annuals appear tired and withered by mid-summer, try trimming them back to encourage a second blooming. Mounding or low-growing annuals, such as petunias, respond well to trimming. Take your garden shears and trim back a quarter or half of the plant growth. New growth will sprout along with a second flush of flowers.

Some annuals have very tall growth and cannot be pinched or trimmed. Instead, remove the main shoot after it blooms and side shoots may develop. Tall annuals, like candle larkspur, require staking with bamboo or other tall, thin stakes. Tie the plant loosely to the stake—strips of nylon hosiery make soft ties that won't cut into the plant. Stake bushy plants with twiggy branches or tomato cages. Insert the twigs or cages around the plant when it is small and it will grow to fill in and hide the stakes.

Tuberous begonia can be overwintered.

ANNUALS FROM PERENNIALS

Many of the plants grown as annuals are actually perennials, such as geraniums, that originate in warmer climates and are unable to survive colder winters. Other plants grown as annuals are biennials, such as forget-me-nots, which are started very early in the year to allow them to grow and flower in a single season. These perennials and biennials are listed as such in the text. There are several techniques you can use in order to keep these plants for more than one summer.

Tropical perennials are given special treatment to help them survive winter, or they are simply brought inside and treated as houseplants in the colder months. A process similar to hardening off is used to acclimatize plants to an indoor environment.

Plants such as geraniums, black-eyed Susan vine and heliotrope, which are grown in the sun all summer, are gradually moved to shady garden spots. This gives them a chance to develop more efficient leaves, capable of surviving in limited light.

Perennials with tuberous roots can be stored over winter and replanted in late winter or early spring. Plants such as dahlias, tuberous begonias and four o'clock flower can be dug up in fall after the plant dies back but before the ground freezes. Shake the loose dirt away from the roots and let them dry out a bit in a cool dark place. Once they are dry, the rest of the soil should brush away. Dust the tubers with an anti-fungal powder (found at garden centres) before storing them in moist peat moss or coarse sawdust. Keep them in a cool, dark, dry place that doesn't freeze. Pot them if they start to sprout and keep them in a bright window and in moist soil. By late winter or early spring they should be potted so they will be ready for spring planting.

Cuttings can be taken from large or fast-growing plants such as licorice plant and black-eyed Susan vine. Grow late-summer cuttings over winter for new spring plants. If winter storage sounds like too much work, replace them each year and leave the hard work to the growers.

Four o'clock Flower

PESTS & DISEASES

New annuals are planted each spring and often different species are grown each year. These factors make it difficult for pests and diseases to find their preferred host plants and establish a population. However, because annual species are often grown together in masses, any problems that set in over summer are likely to attack all the plants.

For many years pest control meant spraying or dusting, with the goal to eliminate every pest in the landscape. A more moderate approach advocated today is IPM (Integrated Pest Management or Integrated Plant Management). The goal of IPM is to reduce pest problems to levels at which only negligible damage is done. Of course, you, the gardener, must determine what degree of damage is acceptable to you. Consider whether a pest's damage is localized or covers the entire plant. Will the damage kill the plant or is it only affecting the outward appearance? Are there methods of controlling the pest without chemicals?

Chemicals are the last resort, because they may do more harm than good. They can endanger the gardener and his or her family and pets, and they kill as many good as bad organisms, leaving the whole garden vulnerable to even worse attacks. A good IPM program includes learning about your plants and the conditions they need for healthy growth, what pests might affect your plants, where and when to look for those pests and how to control them. Keep records of pest

Tidying up the garden

and keeping your soil healthy, with plenty of organic matter, are just two of the cultural controls you can use to keep pests manageable. Choose resistant varieties of annuals that are not prone to problems. Space the plants so that they have good air circulation around them and are not stressed from competing for light, nutrients and space. Remove plants from the landscape if they are decimated by the same pests every year. Remove and burn or take to a permitted dump site diseased foliage and branches, and prevent the spread of disease by keeping your gardening tools clean and by tidying up fallen leaves and dead plant matter at the end of every growing season.

Physical controls are generally used to combat insect problems. An example of such a control is picking insects off plants by hand, which is not as daunting as it may seem if you catch the problem when it is just beginning. Large, slow insects are particularly easy to pick off. Other physical controls include barriers that stop insects from getting to the plant, and traps that catch or confuse insects. Physical control of diseases often necessitates removing the infected plant part or parts to prevent the spread of the problem.

Biological controls make use of populations of predators that prey on pests. Animals such as birds, snakes, frogs, spiders, lady beetles and certain bacteria can play an important role in keeping pest populations at a manageable level. Encourage these creatures to take up permanent residence in your garden. A birdbath and birdfeeder will encourage birds to

damage because your observations can reveal patterns useful in spotting recurring problems and in planning your maintenance regime.

There are four steps in effective and responsible pest management. Cultural controls are the most important. Physical controls should be attempted next, followed by biological controls. Resort to chemical controls only when the first three possibilities have been exhausted.

Cultural controls are the gardening techniques you use in the day-to-day care of your garden. Keeping your plants as healthy as possible is the best defence against pests. Growing annuals in the conditions they prefer

enjoy your yard and feed on a wide variety of insect pests. Many beneficial insects are probably already living in your landscape, and you can encourage them to stay by planting appropriate food sources. Many beneficial insects eat nectar from flowers such as the perennial yarrow.

Chemical controls should rarely be necessary, but if you must use them there are some 'organic' options available. Organic sprays are no less dangerous than chemical ones, but they will break down into harmless compounds. The main drawback to using any chemicals is that they may also kill the beneficial insects you have been trying to attract to your garden. Organic chemicals are available at most garden centres and you should follow the manufacturer's instructions carefully. A large amount of insecticide is not going to be any more effective in controlling pests than the recommended amount. Note that if a particular pest is not listed on the package, it will not be controlled by that product. Proper and early identification of pests is vital to finding a quick solution.

Whereas cultural, physical, biological and chemical controls are all possible defences against insects, diseases can only be controlled culturally. It is most often weakened plants that succumb to diseases. Healthy plants can often fight off illness, although some diseases can infect plants regardless of their level of health. Prevention is often the only hope: once a plant has been infected, it should probably be destroyed, in order to prevent the disease from spreading.

Bullfrogs eat many insect pests.

Butterflies in the garden add colour and charm.
Bees are valuable pollinators in the garden (below).

GLOSSARY OF PESTS & DISEASES

Larva eating flowers

Aphids on leaf bottom (above)

Ladybird beetle larvae (below) are common garden predators.

ANTHRACNOSE

Fungus. Yellow or brown spots on leaves; sunken lesions and blisters on stems; can kill plant.

What to Do. Choose resistant varieties and cultivars; keep soil well drained; thin out stems to improve air circulation; avoid handling wet foliage. Remove and destroy infected plant parts; clean up and destroy debris from infected plants at end of growing season.

APHIDS

Tiny, pear-shaped insects, winged or wingless; green, black, brown, red or grey. Cluster along stems, on buds and on leaves. Suck sap from plants; cause distorted or stunted growth. Sticky honeydew forms on surfaces and encourages sooty mould growth.

What to Do. Squish small colonies by hand; disloge them with water spray; spray serious infestations with insecticidal soap; many predatory insects and birds feed on them.

ASTER YELLOWS

Transmitted by insects called leafhoppers. Stunted or deformed growth; leaves yellowed and deformed; flowers dwarfed and greenish; can kill plant.

What to Do. Control leafhoppers with insecticidal soap; remove and destroy infected plants; destroy any local weeds sharing the symptoms.

BEETLES

Many types and sizes; usually rounded in shape with hard, shell-like outer wings covering membranous inner wings. Some are beneficial, e.g., ladybird beetles ('ladybugs'); others, e.g., June beetles, eat plants. Larvae: see Borers, Grubs. Leave wide range of chewing damage: make small or large holes in or around margins of leaves; consume entire leaves or areas between leaf veins ('skeletonize'); may also chew holes in flowers.

What to Do. Pick beetles off at night and drop them into an old coffee can half filled with soapy water (soap prevents them from floating); spread an old sheet under plants and shake off beetles to collect and dispose of them.

BORERS

Larvae of some moths, wasps, beetles; among the most damaging plant pests. Burrow into plant stems, branches, leaves and/or roots; destroy vascular tissue (plant veins and arteries) and structural strength. Worm-like; vary in size and get bigger as they bore through plants. Burrow and weaken stems to cause breakage; leaves will wilt; may see tunnels in leaves, stems or roots; rhizomes may be hollowed out entirely or in part.

What to Do. May be able to squish borers within leaves. Remove and destroy bored parts; may need to dig up and destroy infected roots and rhizomes.

BOTRYTIS BLIGHT

Fungal disease. Leaves, stems and flowers blacken, rot and die.

What to Do. Thin stems to improve air circulation, keep mulch away from base of plant, particularly in spring, when plant starts to sprout; remove debris from garden at end of growing season; do not over-water. Remove and destroy any infected plant parts.

Damage from spittlebug larva (above); treat as for aphids. Leaf miner damage (below)

Ladybird Beetle

BUGS (TRUE BUGS)
Small insects, up to 1 cm (1/2") long; green, brown, black or brightly coloured and patterned. Many beneficial; a few pierce plants to suck out sap. Toxins may be injected that deform plants; sunken areas left where pierced; leaves rip as they grow; leaves, buds and new growth may be dwarfed and deformed.
What to Do. Remove debris and weeds from around plants in fall to destroy overwintering sites. Pick off by hand and drop into soapy water; spray plants with insecticidal soap.

CUTWORMS
Larvae of some moths. About 2.5 cm (1") long; plump, smooth-skinned caterpillars; curl up when poked or disturbed. Usually affect only young plants and seedlings, which may be completely consumed or chewed off at ground level.
What to Do. Create physical barriers from old toilet tissue rolls to make collars around plant bases; push tubes at least halfway into ground.

GRUBS
Larvae of different beetles, commonly found below soil level; usually curled in C-shape. Body white or grey; head may be white, grey, brown or reddish. Problematic in lawns; may feed on plant roots. Plant wilts despite regular watering; may pull easily out of ground in severe cases.
What to Do. Toss any grubs found while digging onto a stone path or patio for birds to devour; apply parasitic nematodes or milky disease spore to infested soil (ask at your local garden centre).

LEAF MINERS
Tiny, stubby larvae of some butterflies and moths; may be yellow or green. Tunnel within leaves leaving winding trails; tunneled areas lighter in colour than rest of leaf. Unsightly rather than health risk to plant.
What to Do. Remove debris from area in fall to destroy overwintering sites; attract parasitic wasps with nectar plants such as yarrow. Remove and destroy infected foliage; can sometimes squish by hand within leaf.

LEAF SPOT
Two common types: one caused by bacteria and the other by fungi. *Bacterial*: small speckled spots grow to encompass entire leaves; brown or purple in colour; leaves may drop. *Fungal*: black, brown or yellow spots; leaves wither.
What to Do. Bacterial infection more severe; must remove entire plant. For fungal infection, remove and destroy infected plant parts. Sterilize removal tools; avoid wetting foliage or touching wet foliage; remove and destroy debris at end of growing season.

MEALYBUGS

Tiny crawling insects related to aphids; appear to be covered with white fuzz or flour. Sucking damage stunts and stresses plant. Mealybugs excrete honeydew that promotes growth of sooty mould. **What to Do.** Remove by hand on smaller plants; wash plant off with soap and water; wipe off with alcohol-soaked swabs; remove leaves with heavy infestations; encourage or introduce natural predators such as mealybug destroyer beetle and parasitic wasps; spray with insecticidal soap. Keep in mind larvae of mealybug destroyer beetles look like very large mealybugs.

MILDEW

Two types, both caused by fungus, but with slightly different symptoms. *Downy mildew:* yellow spots on upper sides of leaves and downy fuzz on undersides; fuzz may be yellow, white or grey. *Powdery mildew:* white or grey powdery coating on leaf surfaces that doesn't brush off. **What to Do.** Choose resistant cultivars; space plants well; thin stems to encourage air circulation; tidy any debris in fall. Remove and destroy infected leaves or other parts.

NEMATODES

Tiny worms that give plants disease symptoms. One type infects foliage and stems; the other infects roots. *Foliar:* yellow spots that turn brown on leaves; leaves shrivel and wither; problem starts on lowest leaves and works up plant. *Root-knot:* plant is stunted; may wilt; yellow spots on leaves; roots have tiny bumps or knots. **What to Do.** Mulch soil, add organic matter, clean up debris in fall. Don't touch wet foliage of infected plants; can add parasitic nematodes to soil. Remove infected plants in extreme cases.

ROT

Several different fungi that affect different parts of the plant and can kill plant. *Crown rot:* affects base of plant, causing stems to blacken and fall over and leaves to yellow and wilt. *Root rot:* leaves yellow and plant wilts; digging up plant will show roots rotted away. **What to Do.** Keep soil well drained; don't damage plant if you are digging around it; keep mulches away from plant base. Destroy infected plant if whole plant affected.

RUST

Fungi. Pale spots on upper leaf surfaces; orange, fuzzy or dusty spots on leaf undersides. **What to Do.** Choose rust-resistant varieties and cultivars; avoid handling wet leaves; provide plant with good air circulation; clear up garden debris at end of season. Remove and destroy infected plant parts.

Garden centipedes are predators.

Snail eating leaf

SLUGS & SNAILS

Slugs lack shells; snails have a spiral shell; both have slimy, smooth skin; can be up to 20 cm (8") long; in Ontario they are smaller, usually no bigger than 4 cm (1 1/2"); grey, green, black, beige, yellow or spotted. Leave large ragged hole in leaves and silvery slime trails on and around plants.

What to Do. Attach strips of copper to wood around raised beds or smaller boards inserted around susceptible groups of plants; slugs and snails will get shocked if they touch copper surfaces. Pick off by hand in the evening and squish with boot or drop in can of soapy water. Spread wood ash or diatomaceous earth (available in garden centres) on ground around plants; it will pierce their soft bodies and cause them to dehydrate.

SOOTY MOULD

Fungus. Thin black film forms on leaf surfaces and reduces amount of light getting to leaf surfaces.

What to Do. Wipe mould off leaf surfaces; control insects like aphids, mealybugs, whiteflies (honeydew left on leaves encourages mould).

SPIDER MITES

Almost invisible to the naked eye; relatives of spiders without their insect-eating habits. Tiny; eight-legged; may spin webs; red, yellow or green; usually found on undersides of plant leaves. Suck juice out of leaves; may see fine webbing on leaves and stems; may see mites moving on leaf undersides; leaves become discoloured and speckled in appearance, then turn brown and shrivel up.

What to Do: Wash off with a strong spray of water daily until all signs of infestation are gone; predatory mites are available through garden centres; spray plants with insecticidal soap.

THRIPS

Difficult to see; may be visible if you disturb them by blowing gently on an infested flower. Yellow, black or brown; tiny, slender; narrow fringed wings. Suck juice out of plant cells, particularly in flowers and buds, causing mottled petals and leaves, dying buds and distorted and stunted growth.

What to Do. Remove and destroy infected plant parts; encourage native predatory insects with nectar plants like yarrow; spray severe infestations with insecticidal soap.

VIRUSES

Plant may be stunted and leaves and flowers distorted, streaked or discoloured. Viral diseases in plants cannot be controlled.

What to Do: Destroy infected plants; control insects like aphids, leafhoppers and whiteflies that spread disease.

WHITEFLIES

Flying insects that flutter up into the air when the plant is disturbed. Tiny; moth-like; white; live on undersides of plant leaves. Suck juice out of plant leaves, causing yellowed leaves and weakened plants; leave sticky honeydew on leaves, encouraging sooty mould growth.

What to Do. Destroy weeds where insects may live. Attract native predatory beetles and parasitic wasps with nectar plants like yarrow; spray severe cases with insecticidal soap. Can make a sticky flypaper-like trap by mounting tin can on stake; wrap can with yellow paper and cover with clear baggie smeared with petroleum jelly; replace baggie when full of flies.

Lygus Bug enjoying annual Cosmos

WILT

If watering hasn't helped a wilted plant, one of two wilt fungi may be at fault. *Fusarium wilt*: plant wilts, leaves turn yellow then die; symptoms generally appear first on one part of plant before spreading to other parts. *Verticillium wilt*: plant wilts; leaves curl up at edges; leaves turn yellow then drop off; plant may die.

What to Do. Both wilts difficult to control. Choose resistant plant varieties and cultivars; clean up debris at end of growing season. Destroy infected plants; solarize (sterilize) soil before replanting (this may help if you've lost an entire bed of plants to these fungi)—contact local garden centre for assistance.

You can make your own insecticidal soap at home. Mix 5 ml (1 tsp.) of mild dish detergent or pure soap (biodegradable options are available) with 1 litre (1 quart) of water in a clean spray bottle. Spray the surface areas of your plants and rinse them well within an hour of spraying.

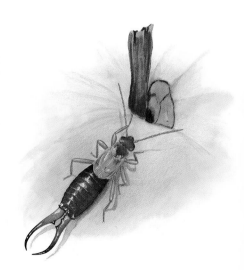

The European Earwig can be good or bad in the garden. It eats dead plant material and other insects, but also can eat flowers.

About This Guide

*T*he annuals in this book are organized alphabetically by their local common names. Additional common names and Latin names appear after the primary reference. Quick identification information on height, spread, and flower colour are the first details given on each plant. At the back of the book there is a **Quick Reference Chart**, a handy guide to planning diversity in your garden.

For each entry, we describe our favourite recommended or alternate species, but keep in mind that many more hybrids, cultivars and varieties are often available. Check with your local greenhouses or garden centres when making your selection. The **Flowers at a Glance** section has a photo of one flower from each entry to allow you to become familiar with the different flowers.

Pests or diseases common to a plant, if any, are listed for each entry. Look in the introduction in the section **Pests & Diseases** for information on how to solve the common problems that can plague your plants.

Because our region is so climatically diverse, we refer to the seasons in only the general sense. The last frost date is specific to your area; refer to the map on p. 13 and consult your local garden centre.

The Annuals

African Daisy
Monarch of the Veldt
Arctotis (Venidium)

Height: 30–60 cm (12–24") **Spread:** 30–40 cm (12–16")
Flower colour: pink, orange, yellow, red or white

African daisies have many charms and reward the gardener with cheerful blooms in unusual colours. They grow well in dry conditions and prefer relative cool, a rare combination in Ontario. These plants are still worth trying, though. The popularity of annual gardening has seen the introduction of many plants called 'African Daisy,' so take note of the botanical name before visiting the garden centre.

PLANTING

Seeding: Indoors in early spring; direct sow after last frost.

Planting out: Once soil has warmed.

Spacing: 30–40 cm (12–16").

GROWING

Choose a location in **full sun**. The soil should be **average, moist** and **well drained**. African daisies don't mind sandy soil, and they tolerate drought well, particularly if the weather isn't too hot.

Seeds started indoors should be planted in peat pots or peat pellets to avoid disturbing the roots when the seedlings are transplanted. African daisy seeds do not keep, so purchase or collect new seeds each year. Deadhead to prolong the blooming season.

TIPS

African daisies can be grouped or massed in beds, borders and cutting gardens. They do quite well when grown in planters and other containers. If summers prove too hot for these plants, try a fall crop—sow seeds directly in the garden in mid-summer and enjoy the flowers all fall.

RECOMMENDED

There are several hybrids with striking flowers. **Harlequin Hybrids** grow up to 50 cm (20") tall and spread 30 cm (12") wide. They do not come true from seed and are propagated by cuttings. Flowers may be pink, red, white, orange or yellow.

A. fastuosa (Monarch of the Veldt, Cape Daisy) has bright orange flowers with a purple spot at the base of each petal. It grows 30–60 cm (12–24") tall and spreads 30 cm (12"). **'Zulu Prince'** bears large cream white or yellow flowers with bands of brown and orange at the base of each petal.

A. stoechadifolia **var.** *grandis* (African Daisy) has 8 cm (3") wide blooms that are white with a yellow ring, and the undersides of the petals are pale lavender-blue. The plant has a nice bushy form and grows 60 cm (24") tall and 40 cm (16") wide.

PROBLEMS & PESTS

Watch for aphids, leaf miners, downy mildew and leaf spot.

African daisies make interesting cut flowers, but they close up at night and in rooms that are not very bright.

Ageratum
Floss Flower
Ageratum

Height: 15–60 cm (6–24") **Spread:** 15–30 cm (6–12")
Flower colour: white, pink, mauve or blue

*I*ts compact, uniform habit and soft, fuzzy flower clusters keep Ageratum in demand as an edging plant. New introductions such as 'Pinky Improved,' with dusky pink flowers, and 'Bavaria,' with blue and white bicoloured flowers, offer variations from the classic blue. Combine them with nasturtiums, snapdragons or 'Teddy Bear' sunflowers for a contrast in colour, texture and size.

PLANTING
Seeding: Indoors in early spring; direct sow after last frost.

Planting out: Once soil has warmed.

Spacing: About 10–30 cm (4–12") apart.

GROWING

Ageratum prefers **full sun** but will tolerate partial shade. The soil should be **fertile, moist** and **well drained**.

Don't cover the seeds; they need light to germinate.

These plants don't like to have their soil dry out; a moisture-retaining mulch will cut down on how frequently you have to water them. Don't mulch too thickly or too close to the base of the plant, or the plants may develop crown rot or root rot.

TIPS

The smaller varieties, which become almost completely covered with the fluffy flowerheads, make excellent edging plants for flower beds. They are also attractive grouped in masses or grown in planters. The taller varieties are useful in the centre of a flowerbed and make interesting cut flowers.

Ageratum *is a genus with about 40 species of annuals, perennials and shrubs. Naturalized in many warm areas, they range from tropical South America to warm-temperate North America.*

The original species was a tall, leggy plant that was not considered attractive enough for the annual border but was used in the cutting garden. New cultivars are much more compact, and Ageratum is now a proudly displayed annual.

RECOMMENDED

A. houstonianum forms a large, leggy mound that can grow up to 60 cm (24") tall. Clusters of fuzzy blue, white or pink flowers are held above the foliage. There are many cultivars available; most have been developed to maintain a low compact form that is more useful in the border. **'Bavaria'** grows about 25 cm (10") tall with blue and white bicoloured flowers. **'Blue Hawaii'** is a

compact plant, 15–20 cm (6–8") tall, with blue flowers. **'Pinky Improved'** is a compact plant with subtle, dusky pink flowers. **'Summer Snow'** has white flowers.

PROBLEMS & PESTS

Powdery mildew may become a problem. Be sure to plant Ageratum in a location with good air circulation to help prevent powdery mildew and other fungal problems.

The genus name Ageratum *is derived from Greek and means 'without age,' a reference to the long-lasting flowers.*

Amaranth

Amaranthus

Height: 90–150 cm (3–5') **Spread:** 30–75 cm (12–30")
Flower colour: red, yellow or green; flowers inconspicuous in some species

This huge group of plants includes several popular garden plants. Love-lies-bleeding is a beautiful plant with a gruesome name. The long, rope-like clusters of flowers dangle to the ground in shades of red, maroon or green. Joseph's Coat is bold and dramatic. Its foliage is bronzed green, flaming red or variegated with brilliant shades of orange, yellow and gold. A little goes a long way when incorporating these plants into the border.

Several species of Amaranthus *are used as potherbs and vegetables because the leaves are high in protein; other species are grown as grain crops.*

PLANTING

Seeding: Indoors about three weeks before last frost; direct sow once soil has warmed.

Planting out: Once soil has warmed.

Spacing: 30–60 cm (12–24").

GROWING

A location in **full sun** is preferable. The soil should be **poor to average** and **well drained**. Seeds started indoors should be planted in peat pots or pellets to avoid disturbing the roots when transplanting them.

Don't give these plants rich soil or over-fertilize them, or their growth will be tall and soft and prone to falling over. Joseph's Coat will lose some of its leaf colour when over-fertilized; its colours will be more brilliant in poorer soil. Love-lies-bleeding self-seeds and can show up year after year. Unwanted plants are easy to uproot when they are young.

A. caudatus

A. tricolor (above and below)

TIPS

Love-lies-bleeding is attractive grouped in borders or in mixed containers, where it requires very little care or water over summer. Joseph's Coat is a bright and striking plant that is best used as an annual specimen plant in a small group rather than in a large mass planting, where it quickly becomes overwhelming. It is also attractive when mixed with large foliage plants in the back of a border.

RECOMMENDED

A. caudatus (Love-lies-bleeding) has erect stems and long, fluffy red, yellow or green drooping flowers that can be air dried. It grows 90–150 cm (36–60") tall and 45–75 cm (18–30") wide.

A. tricolor (Joseph's Coat) is a bushy, upright plant with brightly coloured foliage. It grows up to 1.5 m (5') tall and spreads 30–60 cm (12–24"). The foliage is variegated and can be green, red, bronze, chocolatey purple, orange, yellow or gold. **'Illumination'** has hanging foliage in crimson and gold and inconspicuous flowers. It grows 1.2 m (4') tall and 30 cm (12") wide.

PROBLEMS & PESTS
Cold nights below 10° C (50° F) will cause leaf drop. Rust, leaf spot, root rot, aphids and some viral diseases are potential problems.

A. caudatus (above and below)

Angel's Trumpet
Datura, Trumpet Flower
Datura (Brugmansia)

Height: 90–300 cm (36–120") **Spread:** 90–150 cm (36–60")
Flower colour: white, yellow or purple

*T*he exotic angel's trumpets are claiming more space in Ontario gardens. Sprawling sublimely on the ground or growing at a breathless pace in containers, they add fragrance and a tropical dimension to our cold climate gardens. Some varieties with double flowers and frilly edges look like the edges of old-fashioned petticoats.

PLANTING
Seeding: Slow to germinate. Start indoors in mid-winter. May not grow to flowering size until late summer.

Planting out: Once soil has warmed and frost danger has passed.

Spacing: 60–90 cm (24–36") apart.

GROWING

Angel's trumpets prefer **full sun**. Soil should be **fertile, moist** and **well drained**. Don't allow plants to completely dry out, particularly during hot, dry weather. Plants recover quickly from wilting when watered.

Propagate seeds indoors in early or mid-winter. Have patience as the seeds can be slow to germinate. Keep the soil moist but not soggy. The popularity of these plants has been increasing in recent years, and many garden centres carry started plants.

TIPS

Angel's trumpets tend to flower at night. Grow these plants where you will be able to enjoy their intoxicating scent in the evening—near a patio or in a large container on a deck. If angel's trumpets are planted under an open window, the scent will carry into the room. They are attractive when used as specimen plants or in groups.

B. 'Charles Grimaldi' (below)

RECOMMENDED

The genus to which these plants belong varies. They may be attributed to *Datura* or *Brugmansia*. The two genera are closely related. In general the herbaceous annuals and perennials are classified as *Datura* while the woody plants are classified as *Brugmansia*. This is only slightly helpful because many of the woody plants are treated as tender annuals or perennials in Ontario. Don't worry too much about the names; if you find a plant you like, go ahead and try it.

B. aurea (D. aurea) is a woody plant that can be grown indoors in a cool bright room in winter and outdoors in summer. When grown outdoors, it bears bright yellow or white, scented flowers all summer. In the tropics this plant could grow as tall as 9 m (30'), but in a container or border it will rarely grow taller than 1.5 m (5'). Growth can be controlled by trimming.

B. candida is a woody plant that can be grown in a bright room indoors in winter and moved outdoors in summer. In a container it rarely grows over 3 m (10'). Trim it back to keep the size you want. It bears fragrant, white, trumpet-shaped flowers that may open only at night. **'Grand Marnier'** has apricot-yellow flowers.

B. **'Charles Grimaldi'** is another woody plant. The large, funnel-shaped, pendulous flowers are lemon yellow. This is an excellent container plant for a patio or deck.

Angel's trumpets are in the same family as tomatoes, potatoes, peppers and nightshade plants. As with many other plants in this family, angel's trumpets are poisonous and people have died from eating them.

D. x *hybrida* (*B.* x *hybrida*) includes several hybrid plants of uncertain parentage. **'Angel's Trumpets'** ('Angel') bears white flowers edged with pale pink. The hybrids in the **'Queen'** series are commonly available, often offered in seed catalogues. **'Golden Queen'** has double, yellow flowers. **'Purple Queen'** has double flowers; the inner petals are white and the outer petals are purple.

D. *innoxia* (*D. meteloides*) is a small tender perennial grown as an annual. It grows 1 m (3'). The flowers are white, pink or lavender.

PROBLEMS & PESTS

Problems with whiteflies, spider mites and mealybugs are possible, though more likely on plants grown indoors.

Baby's Breath

Gypsophila

Height: 30–90 cm (12–36") **Spread:** 30–60 cm (12–24")
Flower colour: white, pink or mauve

*B*aby's Breath gives a sense of airiness, light and movement to the garden. It works well in a mixed border where it acts as a mediator between bolder plants, much as it does in cut flower arrangements. Combine with red geraniums, African Marigold or red salvia to temper the bright colours of these flowers.

PLANTING

Seeding: Indoors in late winter; direct sow from mid-spring to early summer.

Planting out: Mid-spring.

Spacing: 20–45 cm (8–18").

GROWING

Baby's Breath grows best in **full sun**. The soil should be of **poor fertility**, and it should be **light, sandy** and **alkaline**. Don't space the seedlings too far apart. The plants will flower more profusely if slightly crowded. Individual plants are short lived, so sow more seeds every week or two until early summer to encourage a longer blooming period. Allow the soil to dry out between waterings.

TIPS

The clouds of flowers are ideal for rock gardens, rock walls, mixed containers or for mixing in borders with bold-coloured flowers. Baby's Breath is native to the northeastern Mediterranean and looks very good in a Mediterranean-style garden.

RECOMMENDED

G. elegans forms an upright mound of airy stems, foliage and flowers. The plant grows 30–60 cm (12–24") tall. The flowers are usually white but can have pink or purple veining that gives the flowers an overall appearance of colour. **'Covent Garden'** has very large white flowers and grows to 50–90 cm (20–36") tall. **'Gypsy Pink'** bears double or semi-double pink flowers. These compact plants grow about 30 cm (12") tall.

PROBLEMS & PESTS

Most of the more common problems are forms of fungal disease and can be avoided by not over-watering the plants and not handling them when they are wet. Leafhoppers can infect plants with aster yellows.

Baby's Breath makes a wonderful addition to flower bouquets. The sprays of flowers can also be dried and used in fresh or dried arrangements.

Bachelor's Buttons
Cornflower, Blue-Bottle
Centaurea

Height: 30–100 cm (12–39") **Spread:** 15–60 cm (6–24")
Flower colour: blue, red, pink, white or violet

I find the flowers of Bachelor's Buttons intriguing at all stages. Before the flowers begin to open, the scales of the tight buds form a diamond pattern. I remember observing a patch of these flowers, some fully open, some just emerging, as they were visited by insects with shimmery, metallic wings. The simple charm of Bachelor's Buttons makes up for their rangy habit.

PLANTING
Seeding: Direct sow in mid-spring or start indoors in late winter.

Planting out: Around last frost.

Spacing: 30 cm (12") apart.

*The Latin name means
'century' and refers to the
folklore that this plant can
live for a hundred years—
it re-seeds easily and outgrows
most pest problems.*

GROWING

Bachelor's Buttons will do best in **full sun. Fertile, moist, well-drained** soil is preferable, but any soil is tolerated. Light frost won't harm the plants.

Seed started indoors should be planted in peat pots or pellets to avoid disturbing roots during transplanting. Shear spent flowers and old foliage in mid-summer for fresh new growth. Deadheading prolongs blooming.

TIPS

Bachelor's Buttons is a great filler plant in a mixed border, wildflower or cottage style garden. It is attractive when used in masses or small groups. Grow Bachelor's Buttons mixed with other plants—as the Bachelor's Buttons fade, the other plants can fill in the space they leave.

RECOMMENDED

C. cyanus is an upright annual that grows 30–90 cm (12–36") tall and

spreads 15–60 cm (6–24"). The flowers of this plant are most often blue but can be shades of red, pink, violet or white. Plants in the **'Boy'** series grow up to 100 cm (39") tall and have large, double flowers in many colours. **'Florence'** is a compact, dwarf cultivar that grows 30–45 cm (12–18") tall and has flowers in various colours.

PROBLEMS & PESTS

Aphids, downy mildew and powdery mildew may cause problems.

Bacopa

Sutera

Height: 8–15 cm (3–6") **Spread:** 30–50 cm (12–20")
Flower colour: white or lavender

The introduction of this plant to North America is one of the reasons mixed containers and hanging moss baskets have become so popular. Along with Licorice Plant, Fan Flower and Sweet Potato Vine it serves as an excellent filler plant. It adds the perfect finishing touch to any mixed planting with dense, cascading growth; neat, scalloped, heart-shaped leaves and beautiful, tiny, delicate flowers of white or pale mauve.

PLANTING
Seeding: Not recommended.

Planting out: Once soil has warmed up.

Spacing: 30 cm (12").

GROWING

Bacopa grows equally well in **full sun** or **partial shade**. The soil should be of **average fertility, humus rich, moist** and **well drained**. Don't allow this plant to completely dry out; the leaves will die quickly if they become dry. Cutting back the dead growth may encourage new shoots to form.

TIPS

Bacopa is a popular plant for hanging baskets, mixed containers and window boxes. It will form an attractive spreading mound in a rock garden, but it will need to be watered regularly.

RECOMMENDED

S. cordata is a compact, trailing plant that bears small white flowers all summer. **'Lavender Showers'** forms a dense mound of heart-shaped leaves with scalloped edges and bears tiny, star-shaped, lavender flowers along its neat, trailing stems. **'Olympic Gold'** has gold-variegated foliage with white flowers. **'Snowflake,'** one of the first cultivars available, bears white flowers. **'Giant Snowflake'** is a more vigorous development of 'Snowflake.'

PROBLEMS & PESTS

Whiteflies and other small insects can become a real menace on this plant, because the tiny leaves and dense growth are perfect hiding spots for them.

Bacopa is a perennial that is grown as an annual outdoors. It will thrive as a houseplant in a bright room.

Begonia
Begonia

Height: 15–60 cm (6–24") **Spread:** 15–60 cm (6–24")
Flower colour: pink, white, red, yellow, orange, bicoloured or picotee

I saw 'Non-stop' trailing begonias transform a yard that was densely shaded by trees into a fairy-tale grotto. The begonias were planted in big terra cotta pots placed around birches and other trees in the yard. The begonias looked like delicate, softly coloured bracelets circling the tree trunks. If they started suffering from too little light, they were moved into a brighter position for a brief period.

PLANTING
Seeding: Indoors in early winter.

Planting out: Once soil has warmed.

Spacing: According to spread of variety.

GROWING

Light or partial shade is best, although some of the new varieties of wax begonia are sun tolerant if their soil is kept moist. The soil should be **fertile,** rich in **organic** matter and **well drained** with a **neutral or acidic** pH. Allow the soil to dry out slightly between waterings, particularly for tuberous begonias.

Begonias can be tricky to grow from seed. Keep the soil surface moist but not soggy, do not cover the seeds and maintain daytime temperature at 21–27° C (70–80° F) and night temperature above 10° C (50° F). Begonias can be potted individually once they are large enough to handle and they have three or four leaves.

Tubers can be purchased in early spring and started indoors. The tubers of tuberous begonias can also be uprooted when the foliage dies back and stored in slightly moistened peat moss over winter. The tuber will sprout new shoots in late winter and can be potted for another season.

TIPS

All begonias are useful for shaded garden beds and planters. The trailing tuberous varieties can be used in hanging baskets and along rock walls where the flowers can cascade over the edges. Wax begonias have a neat rounded habit that makes them

B. x tuberhybrida (above), *B. semperflorens* (below)

B. semperflorens

Wax begonias are the ideal flower for lazy gardeners because they will continue to bloom all summer, even without deadheading.

B. x tuberhybrida

particularly attractive as edging plants. They can also be paired with roses and geraniums in a front-yard bed for a formal look.

Wax begonias can be dug out of the garden before the first frost and grown as houseplants in winter in a bright room.

RECOMMENDED

B. semperflorens (wax begonias) have pink, white, red or bicoloured flowers and green, bronze, reddish or white-variegated foliage. The plants are 15–35 cm (6–14") tall and 15–60 cm (6–24") wide. Plants in the **'Ambassador'** series are heat tolerant and have dark green leaves and white, pink or red flowers. **'Senator'** series plants are heat tolerant and have bronzed leaves and red, pink or white flowers.

B. x tuberhybrida (tuberous begonias) are generally sold as tubers. The flowers come in many shades of red, pink, yellow, orange or white. They

can also have the characteristic of picotee (commonly associated with carnations), with the margins of the flower coloured differently from the main petal. The plants are 20–60 cm (8–24") tall and wide. **'Non-stop'** series begonias can be started from seed. They grow about 30 cm (12") tall with an equal spread; their double and semi-double flowers come in pink, yellow, orange, red and white. ***B. x t. pendula* 'Chanson'** are attractive pendulous begonias and have flowers in many bright shades.

PROBLEMS & PESTS

Problems with mealybugs, powdery mildew, whiteflies, leaf spot, stem rot and *Botrytis* blight can occur.

Begonias have attractive and colourful foliage. Use the dark-leaved forms of wax begonias for splashes of contrasting colour next to a silver-leaved lamium or grey-leaved Licorice Plant.

B. semperflorens

Bells-of-Ireland

Moluccella

Height: 60–90 cm (24–36") **Spread:** 25 cm (10")
Flower colour: green

I remember being fascinated by this plant as a new gardener and attempting to seed it in my garden. Unfortunately it didn't reach maturity. Now looking at its growing needs, I see that perhaps I should have watered it more frequently. Bells-of-Ireland is used by florists because it adds visual curiosity with its unusual shell-like, green bracts.

PLANTING

Seeding: Indoors in mid-winter or direct sow in mid-spring.

Planting out: After last frost.

Spacing: 30 cm (12").

GROWING

Bells-of-Ireland prefers to grow in **full sun** but will tolerate partial shade. The soil should be of **average or good fertility, moist** and **well drained**. When seeding, don't cover the seeds because they need light to germinate. These plants are prone to self-seeding. Seedlings resent transplanting, and this plant generally develops better when its seeds are sown directly into the garden.

TIPS

Use Bells-of-Ireland at the back of a border where the green spikes will create an interesting backdrop for more brightly coloured flowers.

The tall stems may need staking in windy locations.

RECOMMENDED

M. laevis is an upright plant that bears spikes of creamy white inconspicuous flowers. The interesting feature of these plants is the large green shell-like cup that encircles each flower. The species is generally grown and cultivars are rarely offered.

Contrary to what the name implies, these plants are native to the Middle East, not to Ireland.

These plants are popular in fresh or dried flower arrangements. When hung upside down to dry, the green cups become white or beige and papery.

Black-Eyed Susan
Coneflower
Rudbeckia

Height: 25–90 cm (10–36") **Spread:** 30–45 cm (12–18")
Flower colour: yellow, orange, red or sometimes bicoloured;
with brown or green centres

Without the generous flowering of Black-eyed Susan, many gardens would look glum during summer. I remember a somber-looking Victorian house in the Ontario countryside cheered by a front yard completely overrun by plantings of 'Gloriosa Daisy.' Painters would make a pilgrimage every year to capture the scene on canvas.

PLANTING

Seeding: Indoors in late winter; direct sow in mid-spring.

Planting out: Late spring.

Spacing: 45 cm (18").

GROWING

Black-eyed Susan grows equally well in **full sun** or **partial shade**. Soil should be of **average fertility, humus rich, moist** and **well drained**. This plant tolerates heavy clay soil and hot weather. If it is growing in loose, moist soil, Black-eyed Susan may re-seed itself.

'Irish Eyes' (above), *R. hirta* (below)

This tough flower has long-lasting blooms that keep fall flowerbeds bright.

Gloriosa Daisy Mix

TIPS

Black-eyed Susan can be planted individually or in groups. Use these flowers in beds and borders, large containers, meadow plantings and wildflower gardens. They will bloom well, even in the hottest part of the garden.

Keep cutting the flowers to promote more blooming. Black-eyed Susan makes a long-lasting vase flower.

R. hirta is a perennial that is grown as an annual. It is not worth trying to keep over winter because it grows and flowers quickly from seed.

RECOMMENDED

R. hirta forms a bristly mound of foliage and bears bright yellow daisy-like flowers with brown centres in summer and fall. **'Gloriosa Daisy'** grows up to 90 cm (36") tall and has large flowers, up to 15 cm (6") across, in warm shades of gold and brown. **'Indian Summer'** has huge flowers, 15–25 cm (6–10") across, on sturdy stems 90 cm (36") tall or taller. **'Irish Eyes'** plants grow up to 75 cm (30") tall and have single flowers with a green centre. **'Toto'** is a dwarf cultivar that grows 25–30 cm (10–12") tall, small enough to include in planters.

PROBLEMS & PESTS

Good air circulation around plants will help prevent fungal diseases such as powdery mildew, rust and downy mildew. Aphids can also cause the occasional problem.

Black-eyed Susan, with its bright flowers, is a native plant that makes an excellent addition to wildflower and natural gardens.

'Irish Eyes'

Black-Eyed Susan Vine

Thunbergia

Height: over 1.5 m (5')
Spread: can be trained to spread as much as desired
Flower colour: yellow, orange or cream white; usually with dark centres

*B*lack-eyed Susan Vine is a very useful flowering vine that behaves well in containers. Simple flowers dot this vigorous vine, giving it a cheerful, welcoming appearance. I put it in a pot by the front door and train it up a net to frame the doorway. It softens the architecture of the house without impeding traffic.

PLANTING

Seeding: Indoors in mid-winter; direct sow in mid-spring.

Planting out: Late spring.

Spacing: 30–45 cm (12–18").

GROWING

Black-eyed Susan Vine grows well in **full sun, partial shade** or **light shade**. Grow in **fertile, moist** and **well drained** soil that is high in **organic** matter.

TIPS

Black-eyed Susan Vine can be trained to twine around fences and walls as well as up trees and over shrubs. It is also attractive trailing down from the top of a rock garden or rock wall or growing in mixed containers and hanging baskets. It can be brought into the house over winter then returned to the garden the following spring—it is a perennial treated as an annual.

These vines can be quite vigorous and may need to be trimmed back from time to time, particularly if the plant is brought inside for winter. To bring in for winter, acclimatize the plant to the lower light levels by gradually moving it to more shaded locations. Keep it in a bright room out of direct sunlight for winter. The following spring, the plant should be hardened off before being moved outdoors.

RECOMMENDED

T. alata is a vigorous, twining climber. It bears yellow flowers, often with dark centres, in summer and fall. **'Susie'** is a commonly found series that bears large flowers in yellow, orange or white.

Fashion wire frames into any shape to grow Black-eyed Susan Vine into whimsical topiary.

The blooms are actually trumpet shaped with the dark centres forming a tube. This plant also makes an excellent hanging plant.

Blanket Flower

Gaillardia

Height: 30–90 cm (12–36") **Spread:** 30–60 cm (12–24")
Flower colour: red, orange or yellow, often in combination

*T*his member of the daisy family captures the colour and warmth of summer. Blanket Flower, with its variegated yellow, orange and rust-brown flowers, is reminiscent of the colours in a Navajo blanket. Use this drought-tolerant plant in the part of the garden you always forget to water.

PLANTING

Seeding: Indoors in late winter; direct sow in mid-spring.

Planting out: Mid- to late spring.

Spacing: 30 cm (12").

GROWING

Blanket Flower prefers **full sun**. The soil should be of **poor or average fertility, light, sandy** and **well drained**. The less water this plant receives, the better it will do. Don't cover the seeds because they need light to germinate. They also require warm soil.

TIPS

Blanket Flower has an informal, sprawling habit that makes it a perfect addition to an informal cottage garden or mixed border. Being drought tolerant, it is well suited to exposed, sunny slopes, where it can help retain soil while more permanent plants are growing in.

Plant Blanket Flower in a location where it will not get watered with other plants.

Deadhead to encourage more blooms.

RECOMMENDED

G. pulchella forms a basal rosette of leaves. The daisy-like flowers are red with yellow tips. The plants grow 45–90 cm (18–36") tall with a spread of 30–60 cm (12–24"). **'Plume'** series has double flowerheads in vibrant shades of red or yellow. This dwarf plant grows about 30 cm (12") tall, with an equal spread, and blooms for a long time.

The multi-coloured petals on these flowers add a fiery glow to cottage gardens and meadow plantings.

PROBLEMS & PESTS

Possible problems include powdery mildew, leafhoppers, aster yellows, bacterial and fungal leaf spot and rust. If you avoid over-watering, most problems will not become serious.

Blue Lace Flower

Trachymene

Height: 60 cm (24") **Spread:** 20–30 cm (8–12")
Flower colour: pale lavender-blue or white

Blue Lace Flower is a dainty member of the carrot family—it is easy to see its resemblance to Queen Anne's Lace. It looks like it has moved from the roadside into the garden with a few improvements along the way. It combines well with other natural-looking flowers such as the perennial yarrow or annuals Scabiosa, Bachelor's Buttons and Shirley Poppy.

PLANTING

Seeding: Indoors in late winter; direct sow once soil has warmed.

Planting out: After last frost.

Spacing: 30 cm (12").

GROWING

Blue Lace Flower prefers a **sheltered location** in **full sun** that isn't too hot. It enjoys cool night temperatures. The soil should be of **average fertility, light** and **well drained**.

Sowing the seeds directly into the garden is preferable because the seedlings dislike having their roots disturbed. If you do start them indoors, sow the seeds in individual peat pots. The seeds can be slow to germinate.

TIPS

Blue Lace Flower is used in beds and borders and is generally combined with other plants. The plants are quite erect, and with their delicate, feathery foliage they look good in an informal cottage style garden. The flowers are long lasting when used in fresh arrangements.

Insert forked branches around young plants to keep them from flopping over in rain and wind.

RECOMMENDED

T. coerulea is a delicate upright plant that bears light blue, scented flowers. **'Lace Veil'** is a fragrant white cultivar.

Blue Marguerite
Felicia, Blue Daisy
Felicia

Height: 25–60 cm (10–24") **Spread:** 25–60 cm (10–24")
Flower colour: many shades of blue or white with yellow centres

Though Blue Marguerites may sulk in hot humid weather, it is worth trying to grow these blue-flowered beauties. In the right conditions a drift of Blue Marguerite will cool down the hot summer garden. In containers it looks fresh combined with petunias, ivy and lobelia.

PLANTING

Seeding: Indoors in winter; direct sow in mid-summer.

Planting out: After last frost.

Spacing: 30 cm (12").

GROWING

Blue Marguerites like to grow in **full sun**. The soil should be of **average fertility** and **well drained**. These plants do not tolerate heat well. A mid-summer sowing will provide flowers in the cooler temperatures of fall. Take cuttings from the new fall growth of *F. amelloides* to start plants for the following spring. This will save you the uncertainty of starting with seeds or the trouble of trying to overwinter entire large plants.

TIPS

Blue Marguerites, with their sprawling habits, are well suited to rock gardens, bed edges, mixed containers and hanging baskets. The flowers will close at night and on cloudy days.

The key to keeping these plants looking their best is trimming. When they are young, pinch the tips to promote bushiness. Deadhead while they are in flower and cut the plants back when the flowering slows down during the heat of summer. They will revive in the cooler fall weather and produce a second flush of growth and more flowers.

RECOMMENDED

F. amelloides forms a rounded, bushy mound and bears flowers of varied shades of blue all summer. This species is a perennial grown as an annual. '**Astrid Thomas**' is a dwarf variety with medium blue flowers. It grows 25 cm (10") tall, with an equal spread. '**Midnight**' has deep blue flowers.

F. heterophylla forms a low mat of greyish-green foliage. It bears blue daisy-like flowers all summer and grows 50–60 cm (20–24") tall, with an equal spread.

PROBLEMS & PESTS

Blue Marguerites are generally trouble free, although aphids cause occasional trouble.

Blue Marguerites are sometimes called kingfisher daisies. The bright blue colour of the flowers is like the plumage of the European kingfisher.

Blue Marguerite will do well as a houseplant if it is grown in a sunny window.

Browallia
Amethyst Flower
Browallia

Height: 20–45 cm (8–18") **Spread:** 20–45 cm (8–18")
Flower colour: violet, blue or white

I am sentimental about Browallia. It was one of the first annuals I planted in my garden because I love blue. Over the years, my confidence in this little plant has not wavered, even though showier annuals now often get more attention. Browallia adds a fine periwinkle blue to shady spots in the garden or to containers. In bright sun the flowers fade.

PLANTING

Seeding: Indoors in late winter.

Planting out: Once soil has warmed.

Spacing: 20–25 cm (8–10").

GROWING

Browallia will tolerate any light conditions from **full sun** to **full shade**. Flower production and colour are best in **partial shade**. Soil should be **fertile** and **well drained**. Do not cover the seeds when you plant them because they need light to germinate. They do not like the cold, so wait several weeks after the last frost before setting out the plants. Pinch tips often to encourage new growth and more blooms.

TIPS

Grow Browallia in mixed borders, mixed containers or hanging baskets.

Browallia can be grown as a houseplant throughout the year or brought indoors at the end of the season to be used as a houseplant during winter.

RECOMMENDED

B. speciosa forms a bushy mound of foliage. This plant grows 20–45 cm (8–18") tall with an equal or narrower spread and bears white, blue or purple flowers all summer. The **'Jingle Bells'** series includes **'Blue Bells'** and **'Silver Bells.'** They vary in size from 20 cm (8") to 30 cm (12") in both height and spread. **'Starlight'** forms a compact mound up to 20 cm (8") high and wide. Its flowers may be light blue, bright blue, purple or white. The **'Troll'** series includes **'Blue Troll'** and **'White Troll,'** which are compact and bushy. They grow about 25 cm (10") tall.

PROBLEMS & PESTS

Browallia is generally problem free. Whiteflies may cause some trouble.

Calendula
Pot Marigold, English Marigold
Calendula

Height: 25–60 cm (10–24") **Spread:** 20–50 cm (8–20")
Flower colour: yellow, orange, cream, apricot or gold

*C*alendulas are bright and charming. All summer and even when the weather turns cool they produce bright, attractive flowers in warm shades of gold, yellow, orange and copper. They have a long and rich history in North America, arriving with the early European settlers and grown for their medicinal and culinary value. The edible flowers have soothing and antiseptic qualities and are decorative.

PLANTING
Seeding: Direct sow in mid-spring; indoors a month or so earlier.

Planting out: Mid-spring.

Spacing: 20–25 cm (8–10").

GROWING

Calendula does equally well in **full sun** or **partial shade**. It likes cool weather and can withstand a light frost. The soil should be of **average fertility** and **well drained**. Young plants are sometimes difficult to find in nurseries because Calendula is quick and easy to grow from seed and that is how most gardeners grow it. A second sowing in mid-summer gives a good fall display. Deadhead to prolong blooming and keep plants looking neat.

TIPS

These informal plants are attractive in borders and mixed into the vegetable patch. They can also be used in mixed planters. These cold-hardy annuals often continue flowering until the ground freezes completely.

Calendula flowers can be cut for arrangements.

RECOMMENDED

C. officinalis is a vigorous, tough, upright plant; it bears single or double daisy-like flowers in a wide range of yellow and orange shades. This plant grows 30–60 cm (12–24") tall, with a slightly lesser spread. **'Bon Bon'** is a dwarf plant that grows 25–30 cm (10–12") tall and comes in all colours. **'Fiesta Gitana'** ('Gypsy Festival') is a dwarf plant with flowers in a wide range of colours. **'Pacific Beauty'** is a larger plant, growing about 45 cm (18") tall. It bears large flowers in varied colours.

PROBLEMS & PESTS

Calendula plants are often trouble free, but they can have problems with aphids and whiteflies, as well as smut, powdery mildew and fungal leaf spot. They usually continue to perform well even when they are afflicted with problems.

Calendula flowers are popular kitchen herbs that can be added to stews for colour and flavouring or brewed into an infusion that can be used to wash minor cuts and bruises.

California Poppy

Eschscholzia

Height: 20–45 cm (8–18") **Spread:** 20–45 cm (8–18")
Flower colour: orange, yellow or red; less commonly pink, violet or cream

A sure cure for melancholy is the sight of California Poppy flowers the colour of orange sherbet. Sprinkle the seeds of this annual in bare places. The simple, sunset-coloured flowers emerge reliably in the poorest soil. California poppies now come in pastel colours too, some with grey foliage.

PLANTING
Seeding: Direct sow in early to mid-spring.

Spacing: 15–30 cm (6–12").

GROWING

California Poppy prefers **full sun** but will tolerate some shade. The soil should be of **poor or average fertility** and **well drained**. With too rich a soil, the plants will be lush and green but will bear few, if any, flowers. This plant is drought tolerant once well established.

Never start this plant indoors because it dislikes having its roots disturbed. California Poppy will sprout quickly when planted directly in the garden. Start seeds in early fall for blooms in spring or in early spring for blooms later in summer.

California Poppy requires a lot of water for germination and development of young plants. Until they are flowering, provide the plants with regular and frequent watering. Once they begin flowering, they are more drought tolerant.

TIPS

California Poppy can be included in an annual border or annual planting in a cottage garden. This plant self-seeds wherever it is planted; it is perfect for naturalizing in a meadow garden or rock garden where it will come back year after year.

RECOMMENDED

E. californica forms a mound of delicate, feathery, blue-green foliage and bears satiny, orange or yellow flowers all summer. This plant grows 20–45 cm (8–18"). **'Ballerina'** has a mixture of colours and semi-double

or double flowers. **'Chiffon'** forms compact plants, up to 20 cm (8"), that bear semi-double flowers in pink and apricot. **'Mission Bells'** bears ruffled double and semi-double flowers in mixed and solid shades of orange, yellow, red, cream and pink. **'Thai Silk'** bears flowers in pink, red, yellow and orange with silky, wavy-edged petals. The compact plants grow 20–25 cm (8–10").

PROBLEMS & PESTS

California Poppies generally have few pest problems, but fungi may trouble them occasionally.

Candytuft
Iberis

Height: 15–30 cm (6–12") **Spread:** 20 cm (8") or more
Flower colour: white, pink, purple or red

Candytuft is a cheerful and carefree garden plant. It fills the spaces between perennials, shrubs and other annuals with clusters of bright flowers. A light shearing in mid-summer to remove the spent flowerheads will encourage a second flush of blooms in late summer.

PLANTING
Seeding: Indoors in late winter; outdoors around last frost.

Planting out: After last frost.

Spacing: 15 cm (6").

GROWING

Candytuft prefers to grow in **full sun**. The soil should be of **poor or average fertility, well drained** and have a **neutral or alkaline** pH.

TIPS

These informal plants can be used on rock walls, in mixed containers or to edge beds.

RECOMMENDED

I. umbellata (Globe Candytuft) has flowers in shades of pink, purple, red or white. The plant grows 15–30 cm (6–12") tall and spreads 20 cm (8") or more. **'Dwarf Fairy'** ('Dwarf Fairyland') is a compact plant that bears many flowers in a variety of pastel shades.

PROBLEMS & PESTS

Keep an eye open for slugs and snails. Caterpillars can also be a problem. In poorly drained soil, fungal problems may develop.

I. umbellata (both photos)

If your candytuft plant seems to be blooming less often as summer progresses, trim it back lightly to promote new growth and more flowers.

Canterbury Bells
Cup-and-Saucer Plant
Campanula

Height: 45–90 cm (18–36"), depending on variety **Spread:** 30 cm (12")
Flower colour: blue, lavender, purple, pink or white

*T*he flowers of Canterbury Bells seem to be out of a fairytale. The nodding bells of white, blue or pink blend well with other cottage garden plants. New cultivars offer double flowers or dwarf forms, giving gardeners a wider range of possible uses for this old-fashioned favourite.

PLANTING
Seeding: Indoors in mid-winter.

Planting out: Early spring.

Spacing: 15–30 cm (6–12").

GROWING

Canterbury Bells prefers **full sun** but will tolerate partial shade. The soil should be **fertile, moist** and **well drained**. This plant will not suffer if the weather cools or if there is a light frost.

When sowing, leave seeds uncovered because they require light for germination. Harden off in a cold frame or on a sheltered porch before planting out. Canterbury Bells transplants easily, even when in full bloom.

Canterbury Bells is actually a biennial treated like an annual. This is why the plants must be started so early in the year. If they are started too late, they will not flower the first year.

TIPS

Planted in small groups, Canterbury Bells looks good in a border or rock garden. The tallest varieties produce good flowers for cutting. Use dwarf varieties in planters.

Canterbury Bells makes a good addition to a cottage garden or other informal garden where its habit of re-seeding can keep it popping up year after year.

RECOMMENDED

C. medium forms a basal rosette of foliage. The pink, blue, white or purple cup-shaped flowers are borne on tall spikes. It grows 60–90 cm (24–36") tall and spreads about 30 cm (12"). **'Bells of Holland'** is a dwarf cultivar. It has flowers in various colours and grows about 45 cm (18") tall. **'Champion'** is a true annual cultivar, flowering much sooner from seed than the species or other cultivars. Blue or pink flowers are available.

PROBLEMS & PESTS

Occasional, but infrequent, problems with aphids, crown rot, leaf spot, powdery mildew and rust are possible.

Cape Marigold
African Daisy
Dimorphotheca

Height: 30–45 cm (12–18") **Spread:** 30 cm (12")
Flower colour: white, orange, yellow or pink; often with brown, orange or purple centres

*C*ape marigolds may be listed as either *Dimorphotheca* or *Osteospermum*. These two genera are closely related, though *Osteospermum* is more commonly grown in Great Britain. Both types have attractive, daisy-like flowers in pastel shades. I once saw white and pale pink flowered varieties combined in a hanging basket, surrounded by a garden of clematis, delphiniums and peonies in full bloom.

PLANTING
Seeding: Indoors in early spring; direct sow after last frost.

Planting out: After last frost.

Spacing: 30 cm (12").

GROWING

Cape marigolds like to grow in **full sun**. The soil should be **light, fertile** and **well drained**. These plants are drought resistant.

TIPS

Cape marigolds are most attractive when planted in groups or masses. Use them in beds and borders. The flowers close at night and on cloudy days, so although they can be cut for flower arrangements, they might close if the vase is in a dark spot in the house.

Cape marigolds do not grow well in wet climates. Plant under the eaves of the house in window boxes or raised beds to protect them from too much rain.

D. pluvialis

Take along your umbrella on days when the flowers of cape marigolds remain closed. The blooms will not open if rain is forecast.

RECOMMENDED

D. pluvialis (Cape Marigold; Rainy Daisy) has white flowers with purple on the undersides and bases of the petals. **'Glistening White'** is a compact plant that bears large, pure white flowers with black centres.

D. **'Salmon Queen'** bears salmon and apricot pink flowers on plants that spread to about 45 cm (18").

D. sinuata (Star of the Veldt) forms a mound of 30–45 cm (12–18"). Yellow, orange, white or pink daisy-like flowers are borne all summer. Cultivars with larger flowers are available.

D. **'Starshine'** is a low, mound-forming cultivar with shiny flowers in pink, orange, white and red with yellow centres.

PROBLEMS & PESTS

Problems are likely to occur only in hot and wet climates. Dry, cool places produce healthy plants that are less susceptible to disease.

Chilean Glory Flower

Eccremocarpus

Height: 3–5 m (10–15') **Spread:** 30 cm (12")
Flower colour: orange-red

Fast-growing annual vines provide creative freedom in the garden. Used as screens, scampering over the ground or climbing up forms, vines have a transforming effect. The Chilean Glory Flower is a vigorous grower. Its hot-coloured, tubular flowers attract hummingbirds.

PLANTING

Seeding: Indoors in late winter, early spring.

Planting out: After soil thaws.

Spacing: 30 cm (12") apart.

GROWING

Chilean Glory Flower requires **full sun**. This a very fast-growing climbing vine. It grows vigorously in **light, well-drained, fertile** soil.

TIPS

This plant must have something to grow on or against. Walls, arbours, tree trunks or fences are perfect places to plant this fast-growing annual that blooms all season long.

RECOMMENDED

E. scaber is a slender vine that becomes completely covered with orange-red, long, tubular flowers. The flower clusters last from late spring until fall. **'Angelia Hybrids'** offer a wider selection of flower colours including red, pink, orange and yellow. **'Tresco'** mixed enjoys hot locations; it bears flowers of yellow, pink or red.

PROBLEMS & PESTS

Spider mites and whiteflies can be a problem indoors, but outdoors, this vine is relatively pest free.

Chilean Glory Flower is wonderful for screening or shading a porch. The flowers are intriguing as they form, open, and then produce the interesting pudgy seedpods.

The genus name is from the Greek words ekkremus *meaning 'hanging' and* karpos *meaning 'fruit,' referring to the hanging pods of the plant.*

China Aster

Callistephus

Height: 15–90 cm (6–36") **Spread:** 25–45 cm (10–18")
Flower colour: purple, blue, pink, red, white, peach or yellow

*C*hina Asters flower for only a month. Staggering the plantings and choosing cultivars intended for a particular time in the summer will provide you with a longer period of bloom. In late summer and fall the warm, muted pinks and purples offer gardeners an alternative to the more common gold tones of the season.

PLANTING

Seeding: Indoors in late winter; direct sow after last frost.

Planting out: Once soil has warmed.

Spacing: 15–30 cm (6–12").

GROWING

China Aster prefers **full sun** but will tolerate partial shade. The soil should be **fertile, evenly moist** and **well drained**. A pH that is **neutral or alkaline** is preferable.

These plants should be started in peat pots or peat pellets, because they don't like having their roots disturbed.

TIPS

The flowers of China Aster put on a bright display when planted in groups. There are three height groups: dwarf, medium and tall. Use the smaller varieties as edging plants and the taller varieties for cutflower arrangements. Tall varieties may require staking in the garden.

RECOMMENDED

C. chinensis is the parent of many varieties and cultivars. **'Comet'** is an early-flowering cultivar, growing about 25 cm (10") tall, with large, double, quilled flowers in white, yellow, pink, purple, red or blue. **'Duchess'** plants are wilt resistant. The sturdy stems, up to 60 cm (24") tall, bear colourful flowers with petals that curve in towards the centre. **'Meteor'** has plants up to 90 cm (36") tall. The large flowers, up to 10 cm (4") across, are bright red with yellow centres. **'Pot 'n' Patio'** is a popular dwarf cultivar that has double flowers and grows 15–20 cm (6–8") tall, with an equal spread. **'Princess'** grows up to 60 cm (24") tall and bears double or semi-double quilled flowers in a wide range of colours.

PROBLEMS & PESTS

Wilt diseases and aster yellows can be prevented by planting China Aster in different locations each year and by planting resistant varieties. Keep China Aster away from calendulas, which are hosts to potentially harmful insects and diseases.

Chinese Forget-Me-Not
Cynoglossum

Height: 30–60 cm (12–24") **Spread:** to 30 cm (12")
Flower colour: blue, sometimes pink or white

A true blue annual for mid-summer, the Chinese Forget-me-not puts on a prolific flower display. Try weaving it through a perennial border to allow the clusters of tiny blue flowers to peek out unexpectedly from among the other plants and to draw attention away from the rather forgettable foliage. You could also seed it through a planting of petunias for a contrast of solid and delicate forms.

PLANTING
Seeding: Indoors early spring; direct sow late spring.

Planting out: Around last frost date.

Spacing: 30 cm (12") apart.

GROWING
Chinese Forget-me-not prefers **full sun** or **partial shade**. Soil should be of **average fertility, moist** and **well drained**. A heavy clay or overly fertile soil will cause floppy, unattractive growth.

TIPS
Chinese Forget-me-not can be used in difficult areas. The foliage of the plants is not exceptionally attractive, and they are best mass planted or used to fill in the space under shrubs and other tall border plants.

This plant self-seeds quite readily and will return for many seasons. Be careful that it doesn't overtake your garden. Removing the flowerheads right before they seed will keep this situation under control.

RECOMMENDED
C. amabile forms an upright plant that branches strongly and bears bright blue flowers in small clusters. **'Blue Showers'** grows about 60 cm (24") tall and bears attractive, light blue flowers. **'Firmament'** ('Firmament Blue') is a compact variety, about 30–45 cm (12–18") tall, with hairy grey leaves. The pendulous flowers are sky blue.

PROBLEMS & PESTS
This plant is subject to root and stem rot and mildew, problems that can be avoided by not over-watering.

Chrysanthemum
Chrysanthemum

Height: 45–90 cm (18–36") **Spread:** 30–45 cm (12–18")
Flower colour: multi-coloured in white, red, yellow or purple

*I*t seems as if almost all the plants that were once grouped with the chrysanthemums have been moved to other genera. Still in the original genus are the florists' chrysanthemums and a few annual species such as Painted Daisy and Crown Daisy. Chrysanthemums grow quickly from seed and when sprinkled into a perennial border will fill in any spaces with bright, colourful flowers.

PLANTING
Seeding: Spring and mid-summer.

Planting out: Spring and late summer.

Spacing: 25 cm (10").

GROWING

Chrysanthemums prefer **full sun** but tolerate partial shade. The soil should be **average** and **well drained**. A second sowing in mid-summer will bring late-season flowers.

TIPS

These flowers are brightly coloured additions to the informal bed or border. Their most common shades are red, yellow, white or purple; the centres, petal bases and petal tips are often banded in different colours.

Deadhead to prolong the blooming period.

RECOMMENDED

C. carinatum (Tricolour Daisy, Painted Daisy) is an upright plant with fleshy, finely divided foliage. It grows about 60 cm (24") tall and spreads 30 cm (12"). The single flowers have banded petals. The bases, centres and tips of the petals are coloured differently. **'Court Jesters'** has many colours, with the petal bases banded in orange or red. **'Rainbow'** series has many colours, with two bands at the petal bases.

C. coronarium (Crown Daisy) is a tall, upright plant with ferny foliage. It grows up to 90 cm (36") tall and spreads up to 45 cm (18"). Single, yellow flowers are borne from late spring to mid-summer. **'Primrose Gem'** bears bright yellow flowers on compact plants that are half the size of the species.

PROBLEMS & PESTS

Aphids love chrysanthemums; wash them off with insecticidal soap or a brisk spray from the garden hose.

Chrysanthemums make long-lasting and popular cut flowers. According to Victorian flower symbolism, a white chrysanthemum represents truth and a yellow chrysanthemum indicates slighted love.

'Court Jesters'

Cockscomb
Celosia, Woolflower
Celosia

Height: 15–90 cm (6–36"), depending on variety **Spread:** usually equal to height
Flower colour: red, orange, yellow, pink or purple

*T*he unusual flowers of Crested Celosia are appreciated by children and sometimes frowned upon by adults. The bright red, orange or yellow, rooster comb-like flowers are unique but can be difficult to place in the garden. Very adventurous gardeners can try a mass planting of them instead of geraniums or marigolds while the more timid can add small groups of them to spots in the garden that need a bit of livening up, such as along the sunny side of an evergreen hedge. Popular alternatives to the ridgy crested types are the softer Plume Celosias.

PLANTING
Seeding: Indoors in late winter; direct sow in mid- to late spring.

Planting out: Once soil has warmed.

Spacing: Depends on variety.

GROWING

A **sheltered spot** in **full sun** is best. The soil should be **fertile** and **well drained** with plenty of **organic** matter worked in. Cockscombs like to be watered regularly.

It is preferable to start cockscombs directly in the garden. If you need to start them indoors, start the seeds in peat pots or pellets and plant them in the garden before they begin to flower. If left too long in pots, cockscombs will suffer stunted growth and won't be able to adapt to the garden. Keep seeds moist while they are germinating and do not cover them.

Use the expected spread of the variety to determine the appropriate spacing. It will usually be between 10 cm (4") and 45 cm (18").

'Startrek'

To dry the plumes, pick the flowers when they are at their peak and hang them upside down in a cool, shaded place.

Plume Celosia

TIPS

Use cockscomb in borders and beds as well as in planters. The flowers are interesting in cut arrangements, either fresh or dried. A mass planting of Plume Celosia is bright and cheerful in the garden. The popular crested varieties work well as accents and as cut flowers.

RECOMMENDED

C. argentea is the species from which both the crested and plume-type cultivars have been developed. The species itself is never grown. **Cristata Group** (Crested Celosia) has blooms that resemble brains or the combs on roosters. This group has many varieties and cultivars. **'Jewel Box'** bears flowers in red, pink, orange, yellow and gold on compact plants 25 cm (10") tall. **Plumosa Group** (Plume Celosia) has feathery, plume-like blooms. This group also has many

varieties and cultivars. **'Century'** has neat bushy plants up to 60 cm (24") tall that spread 45 cm (18") and bear flowers in many bright colours. **'Fairy Fountains'** is a compact plant, 30 cm (12") tall, that bears long-lasting flowers in red, yellow and pink. Another interesting recent development from the species is *C. a.* **'Startrek'** which has bright pink-plumed flowers that radiate out from a central plume.

C. spicata **'Flamingo'** has spikes of pink flowers that fade to white. It grows about 90 cm (36") tall.

PROBLEMS & PESTS

Cockscombs may develop root rot if planted out too early or if over-watered when first planted out. Cool, wet weather is the biggest problem.

Coleus

Solenostemon (Coleus)

Height: 15–90 cm (6–36") **Spread:** usually equal to height
Flower colour: light purple; grown as a foliage plant

*C*oleus went out of fashion at around the same time as disco. Since then enthusiasts have developed the plant with more and more interesting foliage colours, textures and shapes. The current interest in foliage plants, particularly those that are shade tolerant, has brought attention back to Coleus.

PLANTING

Seeding: Indoors in winter.

Planting out: Once soil has warmed.

Spacing: 30 cm (12").

GROWING

Coleus prefers to grow in **light or partial shade**, but it will tolerate full shade if it isn't too dense and full sun if the plants are watered regularly. The soil should be **moist** and **well drained** and of **rich or average fertility**, with lots of **organic** matter.

Place the seeds in a refrigerator for one or two days before planting them on the soil surface. Cold temperatures will assist in breaking their dormancy. They need light to germinate. Seedlings will all be green at first, but leaf variegation will develop as the plants mature.

Coleus is easy to propagate from stem cuttings, and in doing so you can ensure that you have a group of plants with the same leaf markings, shapes or colours. As your seedlings develop, decide which ones you like best, and when they are about three pairs of leaves high, pinch off the tip. The plants will begin to branch out.

Pinch all the tips off regularly as the branches grow to create a very bushy plant from which you

Coleus can be trained to grow into a standard (tree) form by pinching off the side branches as they grow. Once the plant reaches the desired height, pinch from the top.

will be able to take a large number of cuttings. The cuttings should be about three leaf pairs long. Make the cut just below a leaf pair, and then remove the two bottom leaves. Plant the cuttings in pots filled with a soil mix intended for starting seeds. Keep the soil moist but not soggy. The plants should develop roots within a couple of weeks. Because they are from a single original plant, the plants will all have the same markings and same colour.

TIPS

The bold, colourful foliage makes Coleus dramatic when the plants are grouped together in beds and borders and in mixed containers and used as edging plants. The colours of the foliage can fade in bright sun, so choose the lighter yellow and gold-leaved varieties, which don't fade as badly, for sunny spots. Coleus can also be grown indoors as a houseplant in a bright room.

When flowerbuds develop, it is best to pinch them off, because the plants tend to stretch out and are less attractive after they flower.

Although Coleus is a member of the mint family, with the characteristic square stems, it has none of the enjoyable culinary or aromatic qualities.

RECOMMENDED

S. scutellarioides *(Coleus blumei* var. *verschaffeltii)* forms a bushy mound of foliage. The leaf edges range from slightly toothed to very ruffled. The leaves are usually multi-coloured with shades ranging from pale greenish yellow to deep purple-black. The size may be 15–60 cm (6–24"), depending on the cultivar, and the spread is usually equal to the height. There are dozens of cultivars available and many cannot be started from seed. A few interesting cultivars that can be started from seed are the **'Dragon'** series with bright yellow-green margins to the variably-coloured leaves; **'Palisandra'** with velvety, purple-black foliage; **'Scarlet Poncho'** with wine red leaves edged in yellow-green; and the **'Wizard'** series with variegated foliage on compact plants.

PROBLEMS & PESTS

Mealybugs, scale insects, aphids and whiteflies can cause occasional trouble.

The attractive foliage of Coleus may be green, red, purple, pink, yellow, bronze or maroon. It is often variegated with two or more colours.

Coreopsis
Coreopsis

Height: 20–120 cm (8–48") **Spread:** 20–45 cm (8–18")
Flower colour: yellow, red, orange or maroon

*C*oreopsis is a faithful summer annual that delivers high impact for little effort. It blooms dependably, copes with drought and looks at home in a meadow or a formal border. Mix it with Cosmos, poppies, sunflowers and Bachelor's Buttons to create a garden that looks like a meadow of wildflowers.

PLANTING
Seeding: Indoors in mid-winter; direct sow after last frost.

Planting out: After last frost.

Spacing: 20–30 cm (8–12").

GROWING

Coreopsis prefers **full sun**. The soil should be of **rich or average fertility, light** and **well drained**. Poor soil is also tolerated but with somewhat reduced flowering. Good drainage is the most important factor for these drought-tolerant plants.

TIPS

Coreopsis plants look comfortable growing in front of a rustic wooden fence or repeating in clusters in a bed of perennials. They make a beautiful colour combination planted with deep purple coral bells or royal purple heliotrope. Well suited to naturalized meadow plantings, coreopsis can also be used in informal beds and borders where they will flower all season if deadheaded regularly. These plants also produce lovely cut flowers.

Coreopsis plants can be blown over or have their stems broken during heavy rain or high winds. The fine foliage isn't dense enough to hide tomato or peony cages, so use twiggy branches for the seedlings to grow between for support. In very windy spots, it is best to used the dwarf forms of coreopsis.

RECOMMENDED

C. grandiflora forms a clump of stems and foliage. It grows 45–90 cm (18–36") tall, spreads about 45 cm (18") and bears bright yellow, single flowers all summer. **'Early Sunrise'** bears bright yellow double flowers on compact plants that grow about 45 cm (18") tall.

C. tinctoria forms a clump of basal leaves and tall, branching stems with just a few leaves. It grows up to 120 cm (48") tall and spreads up to 45 cm (18"). The flowers are usually bright yellow with dark red bands at the petal bases; flowers in red, orange or brown are also possible. Dwarf cultivars that grow about 20–30 cm (8–12") are also available.

PROBLEMS & PESTS

Slugs, snails and fungal diseases can be problems.

Self-seeding is very likely with these plants, so they may pop up from year to year in the same area if left to their own devices.

'Early Sunrise'

Cosmos
Cosmos

Height: 30–200 cm (12–84") **Spread:** 30–45 cm (12–18")
Flower colour: magenta, rose, pink, purple, white, yellow, orange or scarlet

*C*osmos fit very well in the flower border and mix easily and handsomely with perennials. Their finely cut foliage and blousy daisy-like flowers add movement and light to the garden. The 'Sonata' series is shorter than its parent species and is a good choice for containers. One gardener I know had white 'Sonata' plants in clay pots lining a pathway, providing a feeling of cheerful illumination. In my own garden an orange cosmos turned a mundane corner into something marvellous with its pulsating colour.

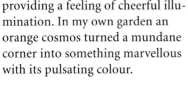

PLANTING
Seeding: Indoors in late winter; direct sow after soil has warmed.

Planting out: After last frost.

Spacing: 30–45 cm (12–18").

GROWING

Cosmos like to be located in **full sun**. Soil should be of **poor or average fertility** and **well drained**. Cosmos are drought tolerant. Over-fertilizing and over-watering can reduce the quantity of flowers produced. Yellow Cosmos will do better if sown directly in the garden. Keep faded blooms cut to encourage more buds. Often, these plants re-seed themselves.

These plants are likely to need staking but are difficult to stake. Save yourself the trouble of staking by planting in a sheltered location or against a fence. You could also grow shorter varieties. If staking can't be avoided, push twiggy branches into the ground when the plants are young and allow them to grow up between the branches to provide support. The branches will be hidden by the mature plants.

Cut flowers make lovely, long-lasting fillers in arrangements.

'Sea Shells'

TIPS

Cosmos are attractive in cottage gardens, at the back of a border or mass planted in an informal bed or border.

RECOMMENDED

C. atrosanguineus (Chocolate Cosmos) has recently become popular among annual connoisseurs for its fragrant, deep maroon flowers that some claim smell like chocolate. The plant is upright, growing to 75 cm (30") tall, but tends to flop over a bit when the stems get too long.

C. bipinnatus (Annual Cosmos) has several cultivars. The flowers come in magenta, rose, pink or white, usually with yellow centres. Old varieties grow 90–180 cm (36–72") tall, while some of the newer cultivars grow 30–90 cm (12–36") tall.

'**Daydream**' has white flowers flushed with pink at the petal bases. '**Sea Shells**' has petals rolled into tubes. '**Sensation**' bears large white or pink flowers. '**Sonata**' bears red, pink or white flowers on compact plants.

C. sulphureus (Yellow Cosmos) has gold, orange, scarlet and yellow flowers. Old varieties grow 2 m (7') tall, and new varieties grow 30–120 cm (12–48") tall. '**Klondike**' are compact plants about 30–60 cm (12–24") tall. Single or semi-double flowers are bright yellow or orange-red. '**Ladybird**' series has compact dwarf plants, 30–35 cm (12–14") tall, that rarely need staking. The foliage is not as feathered as it is in other cultivars.

PROBLEMS & PESTS
Cosmos plants rarely have any problems, but watch for wilt, aster yellows, powdery mildew and aphids.

The name Cosmos is from Greek and means 'beautiful.'

Creeping Zinnia

Sanvitalia

Height: 10–20 cm (4–8") **Spread:** 30–45 cm (12–18")
Flower colour: yellow or orange with dark brown or purple centres

I always regret it if I forget to plant Creeping Zinnia. This undemanding little plant has the naive charm of a miniature Black-eyed Susan. Use it as an informal edging plant or tuck it into containers where it will bubble over edges and loosen up stiff arrangements.

PLANTING

Seeding: Direct sow in mid-spring.

Spacing: 30 cm (12").

GROWING

Creeping Zinnia prefers **full sun**. The soil should be of **average fertility** and **light, sandy** and **well drained**.

Do not cover the seeds when you sow them because they need light to germinate.

TIPS

Creeping Zinnia can be used as an annual groundcover or edging plant. This plant is also dramatic in hanging baskets and in mixed containers.

Creeping Zinnia is one of the easiest annuals to grow. It is also one of the easiest to damage with too much care; over-watering and over-fertilizing can quickly kill the plants.

RECOMMENDED

S. procumbens forms a low mat of foliage up to 20 cm (8") tall. Small yellow or orange, daisy-like flowers with dark centres are borne from summer until long into fall. **'Sprite'** is a mounding plant that has yellow-orange flowers with dark centres. **'Yellow Carpet'** is a low-growing dwarf plant that is up to 10 cm (4") tall and 45 cm (18") wide. It has bright yellow flowers with dark centres.

PROBLEMS & PESTS

Keep Creeping Zinnia from getting hit by a sprinkler system, or you'll have mildew and fungal problems.

The less you do to it, the better this flowering plant will look.

Cup Flower
Nierembergia

Height: 15–30 cm (6–12"). **Spread:** 15–30 cm (6–12").
Flower colour: Blue, purple or white.

Keep Cup Flower out of the scorching summer heat and you will be rewarded with a fine display of winsome little white or purple cup-shaped flowers. This plant is a good choice for containers on a front step or planters on a deck where the flowers can be admired up close. Plant them with tuberous begonias, fuchsia and Sweet Alyssum for a colourful combination of flowers that love partial shade.

PLANTING
Seeding: Indoors in mid-winter.

Planting out: Spring.

Spacing: 15–30 cm (6–12").

GROWING
Cup Flower grows well in **full sun** or **partial shade**. The soil should be **fertile, moist** and **well drained**.

Cup Flower is a perennial used as an annual. During a mild winter in the warmest part of the province it may survive winter. It is easier to start new plants each year than to protect mature plants over winter.

TIPS
Use Cup Flower as an annual groundcover plant. It is also useful for edging beds and borders, in rock gardens and on rock walls and in containers and hanging baskets. It grows best when summers are cool, and it can withstand a light frost.

RECOMMENDED
N. caerulea (*N. hippomanica*) forms a small mound of foliage. This plant bears delicate, cup-shaped flowers in lavender-blue with yellow centres. **'Mont Blanc'** has white flowers with yellow centres. **'Purple Robe'** has deep purple flowers with golden eyes.

PROBLEMS & PESTS
Slugs and snails are likely to be the worst problem for these plants. Because Cup Flower is susceptible to tobacco mosaic virus, don't plant it near any flowering tobacco or tomato plants.

'Mont Blanc'

The former species name hippomanica *is from Greek and means 'drives horses crazy.' Whether they went crazy because they loved to eat it or from actually eating the plant is unclear.*

Cup-and-Saucer Vine
Cathedral Bells
Cobaea

Height: 4.5–7.5 m (15–25') in hot summer areas; 1.8 m (6') in cool summer areas
Spread: may vary **Flower colour:** purple or white

C up-and-saucer Vine produces frilly purple flowers from spring until frost. This climber is vigorous, but not invasive. It is a worthwhile plant to add to the list of annual climbers.

PLANTING
Seeding: Indoors in mid-winter.

Planting out: After last frost.

Spacing: 30 cm (12").

GROWING

Cup-and-saucer Vine prefers **full sun**. The soil should be **well drained** and of **average fertility**. This plant is fond of hot weather and will do best if planted in a sheltered site with southern exposure. Set the seeds on edge when planting them, and barely cover them with soil.

TIPS

Grow up a trellis, over an arbour or along a chain-link fence. Cup-and-saucer Vine requires a sturdy support in order to climb. It uses grabbing hooks to climb so won't be able to grow up a wall without something to grab hold of. It can be trained to fill almost any space.

RECOMMENDED

C. scandens is a vigorous climbing vine from Mexico. It grows 4.5–7.5 m (15–25'); its flowers are creamy green when they open and mature to deep purple. **Var. *alba*** has white flowers.

PROBLEMS & PESTS

This plant may have trouble with aphids.

This interesting vine has sweet-scented flowers that are a cream colour with a green tinge when they open; the flowers darken to purple as they age.

Dahlberg Daisy
Golden Fleece
Thymophylla

Height: 20–30 cm (8–12") **Spread:** 30 cm (12")
Flower colour: yellow or less commonly orange

When this plant is grown well it produces a waterfall of small yellow blossoms on ferny foliage. It is attractive in window boxes. The wild tumble of dainty flowers can even transform the appearance of a metal garden shed. This plant is a good choice in a mixed moss basket where it will flower profusely in the first part of summer and will not be noticed if it fades in the heat of summer.

PLANTING

Seeding: Indoors in mid-winter; direct sow in spring.

Planting out: After last frost.

Spacing: 20–30 cm (8–12").

GROWING

Plant Dahlberg Daisy in **full sun**. Any **well-drained** soil is suitable, although soil of **poor or average fertility** is preferred. Dahlberg Daisy prefers cool summers. In hot climates, it flowers in spring.

Direct-sown plants may not flower until quite late in summer. For earlier blooms, start the seeds indoors. Don't cover the seeds, because they require light to germinate. These attractive plants may self-sow and reappear each year. Trimming the plants back when flowering seems to be slowing will encourage new growth and more blooms.

TIPS

This plant can be used along the edge of borders, along the tops of rock walls or in hanging baskets or mixed containers. In any location where it can cascade over and trail down an edge, Dahlberg Daisy will look wonderful.

RECOMMENDED

T. tenuiloba (*Dyssodia tenuiloba*) forms a mound of ferny foliage. From spring until the summer heat causes it to fade, it produces many bright yellow daisy-like flowers. Trim it back once the flowers fade, and it may revive in late summer as the weather cools.

Dahlberg Daisy has fragrant foliage that some people compare to a lemon-thyme scent, perhaps the origin of the name Thymophylla, *meaning 'thyme-leaf.'*

Dahlia

Dahlia

Height: 20–150 cm (8–60") **Spread:** 20–45 cm (8–18")
Flower colour: purple, pink, white, yellow, orange, red or bicoloured

*S*ome people only dabble in dahlias, while others completely immerse themselves in growing these variable plants. I once saw an entire backyard devoted to dahlias. Each plant was protected by an umbrella (to keep rain from damaging the exhibition-quality flowers) and all the stems were greased with petroleum jelly to stop earwigs. The blooms ranged from button to softball size. If you want to grow dahlias, there will be an enthusiast ready to offer you advice every step of the way.

PLANTING

Seeding: Indoors in mid- to late winter; direct sow in spring.

Planting out: After last frost.

Spacing: 30 cm (12").

GROWING

Dahlias prefer **full sun**. The soil should be **fertile**, rich in **organic** matter, **moist** and **well drained.** Dahlias are tuberous perennials that are treated as annuals. Tubers can be purchased and started early indoors. The tubers can also be lifted in fall, dried and stored over winter in slightly moist peat moss. Pot them and keep them in a bright room when they start sprouting in mid- to late winter.

If there is a particular size, colour or form of dahlia that you want, it is best to start it from tubers of that type. Seed-grown dahlias show a great deal of variation in colour and form, because the seed is generally sold in mixed packages. In order to keep dahlias blooming and attractive, it is essential to remove the spent blooms.

Dahlia flowers are categorized by size, from giants with blooms over 25 cm (10") in diameter to mignons with blooms up to 5 cm (2") in diameter. They are then categorized by type—for example, peony, formal and informal decorative, semi-cactus and waterlily.

Semi-cactus type

Waterlily type

Peony type 'Bishop of Llandaff'

Informal decorative type

Informal decorative type

TIPS

Dahlias make attractive, colourful additions to a mixed border. The smaller varieties make good edging plants and the larger ones make good shrub replacement plants. Varieties with unusual or interestingly formed flowers are attractive specimen plants.

RECOMMENDED

There are many dahlia hybrids. Most must be grown from tubers but there are a few that can be started from seed with good results. Examples include *D.* **'Figaro,'** which forms a round, compact plant 30–40 cm (12–16") tall. The flowers are small, double or semi-double, come in a wide variety of colours, and grow and flower quickly.

This plant looks very good grouped in a border or in containers. *D.* **'Harlequin'** forms compact plants that flower quickly from seed. Flowers are solid or bicoloured, single or semi-double in many shades. Many hybrid seeds are sold in mixed packets based on flower shape, for example, collarette, decorative or peony flowered. Tubers of specific types and colours can be purchased in late winter and early spring.

PROBLEMS & PESTS

There are a few problems a dahlia grower may encounter: aphids, powdery mildew, slugs and earwigs are the most likely. If a worse problem afflicts your dahlias, it may be best to destroy the infected plants and start over.

Informal decorative type

Diascia

Diascia

Height: 25 cm (10")   **Spread:** 50 cm (20")
Flower colour: many different pinks

*T*hough Diascia plants prefer cooler growing conditions, they are very heat tolerant. It is the humidity that causes them to flag during the height of summer. Plant them in a spot with good air circulation and make sure they have some shelter from the afternoon sun, and you may find them to be very forgiving of the humid Ontario summers.

PLANTING

Seeding: Indoors in spring.

Planting out: After the last frost.

Spacing: 45 cm (18").

GROWING

Diascia prefers **full sun**, but does better in **light or partial shade** with **protection from the afternoon sun** during the humid Ontario summers. The soil should be **fertile, moist** and **well drained**. Diascia is generally frost hardy and will bloom well into fall. To promote new blooms, cut back stems after flowering.

Diascia doesn't thrive in high humidity and heat. Plants may fade during the hottest part of summer but will revive and produce flowers as temperatures drop in fall. Diascia is a perennial treated as an annual in most of North America.

TIPS

Diascia is attractive in a rock garden or mass planted in a border. Pinch tips of plants to increase bushiness.

RECOMMENDED

D. barberae is a low-growing plant that bears loose spikes of pink flowers from mid-summer to frost. **'Blackthorn Apricot'** has apricot-coloured flowers and flowerheads that point downwards. **'Pink Queen'** has light, shimmery pink flowers on long, slender stalks.

D. **'Coral Belle'** is a quick-growing hybrid that forms a dense mound of bright green foliage. The flowers are a delicate coral pink.

D. **'Strawberry Sundae'** is a fairly compact plant with trailing stems and bright pink flowers.

PROBLEMS & PESTS

Watch out for snails and slugs.

Dusty Miller

Senecio

Height: 30–60 cm (12–24") **Spread:** equal to height or slightly narrower
Flower colour: yellow or white; grown for silvery foliage

For a while Dusty Miller seemed to fall out of favour. Now, like Coleus, it is popular once again. Dusty Miller makes an artful addition to planters, window boxes and mixed borders where the soft, silvery-grey, deeply lobed foliage brings out the bright colours of other annual flowers.

PLANTING
Seeding: Indoors in mid-winter.

Planting out: Spring.

Spacing: 30 cm (12").

GROWING
Dusty Miller prefers **full sun** but will tolerate light shade. The soil should be of **average fertility** and **well drained**.

TIPS
The soft, silvery, lacy leaves of this plant are its main feature, and it is used primarily as an edging plant. It is also used in beds, borders and containers. The silvery foliage makes a good backdrop to show off the brightly coloured flowers of other plants.

'Silver Dust' (above), 'Cirrus' (below)

Pinch off the flowers before they bloom or they will detract from the foliage.

RECOMMENDED
S. cineraria forms a mound of fuzzy, silvery-grey, lobed or finely divided foliage. Many cultivars have been developed with impressive foliage colours and shapes. **'Cirrus'** has lobed silvery-green or white foliage. **'Silver Dust'** has deeply lobed silvery-white foliage. **'Silver Lace'** has delicate silvery-white foliage that glows in the moonlight.

PROBLEMS & PESTS
Dusty Miller is usually problem free, although it may occasionally suffer from rust. It is best to remove afflicted plants and not grow them again in the same location.

Mix Dusty Miller with geraniums, begonias or cockscomb to really bring out the vibrant colours of these flowers.

Dwarf Morning Glory

Convolvulus

Height: 15–40 cm (6–16") **Spread:** 25–30 cm (10–12")
Flower colour: blue, purple or pink

*D*warf Morning Glory, especially 'Royal Ensign' with its stunning royal blue flowers, deserves a place in every garden. This annual is closely related to the dreaded Bindweed, *Convolvulus repens*, but fortunately Dwarf Morning Glory does not have the unstoppable twining and spreading power of its cousin. Fans of Dwarf Morning Glory love it in baskets and containers and at the front of a border.

PLANTING

Seeding: Indoors in late winter; direct sow in mid- or late spring.

Planting out: Mid- or late spring.

Spacing: 20–30 cm (8–12").

GROWING

Dwarf Morning Glory prefers **full sun**. The soil should be of **poor or average fertility** and **well drained**. This plant may not flower well in rich, moist soil.

Soak the seeds in water overnight before planting them. If starting seeds early indoors, plant them in peat pots to avoid root damage when transplanting.

TIPS

Grow these compact, mounding plants on rock walls or in borders, containers or hanging baskets.

'Royal Ensign'

RECOMMENDED

C. tricolor bears flowers that last only a single day, blooming in the morning and twisting shut that evening. This species grows 30–40 cm (12–16") tall. **'Ensign'** series has low-growing spreading plants growing 15 cm (6") tall. **'Royal Ensign'** has deep blue flowers with white and yellow throats. **'Star of Yalta'** bears deep purple flowers that pale to violet in the throat.

Fan Flower

Scaevola

Height: up to 20 cm (8") **Spread:** up to 90 cm (36") or more
Flower colour: blue or purple

T he introduction of plants such as Fan Flower sparked a new wave of interest in growing annuals when gardeners realized there were more annuals available than they had thought. Fan Flower is heat tolerant, and its trailing nature and masses of purple flowers make it popular for hanging baskets, planters and window boxes.

Frequent pinching and trimming will keep Fan Flower bushy and blooming.

PLANTING

Seeding: Indoors in late winter.

Planting out: After last frost.

Spacing: 60–120 cm (24–48").

GROWING

Fan Flower grows well in **full sun** or **light shade**. The soil should be of **average fertility, moist** and **well drained**. Water regularly, because these plants don't like to completely dry out. They do recover quickly from wilting when they are watered.

This attractive plant is actually a perennial that is too tender to survive winter. Cuttings can be taken during summer and new plants grown indoors to be used the following summer, or a plant can be brought in to be kept in a bright room over winter. Seeds can be difficult to find.

TIPS

Fan Flower is popular for hanging baskets and containers, but it can also be used along the tops of rock walls and in rock gardens where it can trail down. This plant can also make an interesting addition to mixed borders or under shrubs where the long, trailing stems form an attractive groundcover.

RECOMMENDED

S. aemula forms a mound of foliage from which trailing stems emerge. The fan-shaped flowers come in shades of purple, usually with white bases. The species is rarely grown as there are many improved cultivars. **'Blue Wonder'** has long branches that trail, making it ideal for hanging baskets. It can eventually spread 90 cm (36") or more. **'Saphira'** is a new compact variety with deep blue flowers. It spreads about 30 cm (12").

PROBLEMS & PESTS

Whiteflies may cause problems for Fan Flower if the plant becomes stressed from lack of water.

Fan Flower is native to Australia and Polynesia.

Forget-Me-Not
Myosotis

Height: 15–30 cm (6–12") **Spread:** 15 cm (6") or wider
Flower colour: blue, pink or white

*A*fter a long winter we are grateful for the emergence of Forget-me-not and the perfect blue it adds to the spring garden. This plant looks best weaving through plantings of spring bulbs or woodland wildflowers. Though it is short-lived, its habit of self-seeding and appearing each year ensures that you won't forget it.

PLANTING

Seeding: Direct sow in spring; indoors in early spring.

Planting out: Around last frost date.

Spacing: 25 cm (10") apart.

Forget-me-not is a delightful addition to woodland or wet areas as well as wildflower and native plant gardens.

GROWING

Forget-me-not prefers **light or partial shade**, but it will tolerate full sun if the soil stays moist and the weather isn't too hot. The soil should be **fertile, moist** and **well drained**. Adding lots of **organic** matter to the soil will help it retain moisture while maintaining good drainage.

Seeds sown in spring will flower in mid-summer or fall. Forget-me-not is a short-lived perennial that is treated as an annual. It may self-seed if faded plants are left in place until the following spring.

TIPS

Forget-me-not can be used in the front of flowerbeds or to edge beds and borders, in mixed containers and in rock gardens and on rock walls. You can also mix it with naturalized spring-flowering bulbs. This plant thrives in cooler parts of the garden.

RECOMMENDED

M. sylvatica forms a low mound of basal clusters of leaves. Clusters of small blue or white flowers with yellow centres are held on narrow, fuzzy stems above the foliage. '**Ball**' series has flowers in several colours.

PROBLEMS & PESTS

Slugs and snails, downy mildew, powdery mildew and rust may cause occasional trouble.

The common name refers to the way this biennial lives a short life after blooming but then reappears as new seedlings all over the garden.

Four-O'Clock Flower
Mirabilis

Height: 45–90 cm (18–36") **Spread:** 45–60 cm (18–24")
Flower colour: red, pink, magenta, yellow, white or bicoloured

Four-o'clock Flower is often overlooked, but it deserves a place in the garden. This plant is sturdy and shrubby with deep green leaves and showy tubular flowers. The flowers do open late in the day but will last through the next morning and sometimes longer on an overcast day. Rarely can you buy a six-pack of Four-o'clock Flower plants at a nursery, but it is worth growing from seed. You may be the only person on the block with Four-o'clock Flower. Start your own revival.

PLANTING
Seeding: Indoors in late winter; direct sow in mid-spring.

Planting out: Mid-spring.

Spacing: 40–60 cm (16–24").

GROWING
Four-o'clock Flower prefers **full sun** but will tolerate partial shade. The soil should be **fertile**, though any **well-drained** soil will be tolerated.

This plant is a perennial that is treated as an annual, and it may be grown from tuberous roots. Dig up roots in fall and replant in spring to enjoy larger plants.

TIPS
Four-o'clock Flower can be used in beds and borders, containers and window boxes. The flowers are scented, so they are often planted near deck patios or terraces where their scent can be enjoyed in the afternoon and evening.

RECOMMENDED
M. jalapa forms a bushy mound of foliage. The flowers may be solid or bicoloured; often, on a single plant the two colours of the bicolours also appear as solids.

PROBLEMS & PESTS
This plant has very few problems as long as it is given well-drained soil.

Many species of moths are attracted to the flowers of this plant, which may bloom in several colours on a single plant.

Fuchsia

Fuchsia

Height: 15–90 cm (6–36") **Spread:** 15–90 cm (6–36")
Flower colour: pink, red, purple or white; often bicoloured

*I*n hanging baskets the flowers of fuchsias look like ballerinas with frilly tutus. Fuchsias are prized ornamental plants for cool, shady locations in the garden. More cultivars are proving to be heat resistant, which should extend their use in Ontario gardens.

PLANTING

Seeding: Not recommended.

Planting out: After last frost.

Spacing: 30–60 cm (12–24").

Children, and some adults, enjoy popping the fat buds of fuchsia. The temptation to squeeze them is irresistible.

GROWING

Fuchsias are grown in **partial or light shade**. They are generally not tolerant of summer heat, and full sun can be too hot for them. The soil should be **fertile, moist** and **well drained**. Fuchsias need to be well watered, particularly in a hot location or in full sun. Ensure that the soil has good drainage, as the plants can develop rot problems. Fuchsias planted in well-aerated soil with plenty of perlite are almost impossible to over-water. As summer wears on, increase the amount of water given to the plants as the pots and baskets fill with thirsty roots. Fuchsias bloom on new growth; a high-nitrogen plant food encourages new growth.

Fuchsias can be started from seed although the germination rate can be poor and erratic. If you are up for a challenge, start the plants indoors in mid-winter. Ensure that the soil is warm, at 20–24° C (68–75° F). Seeds can take from two weeks to two months to sprout. Plants will start to flower only when the days have more than 13 hours of light. It may be late summer before you see any reward for your efforts.

'Deep Purple'

'Snowburner'

Although fuchsias are hard to start from seed, they are easy to propagate from cuttings. Snip off 15 cm (6") of new tip growth, remove the leaves from the lower third of the stem and insert the cuttings into soft soil or perlite. Once rooted and potted, the plants will bloom all summer.

TIPS

The upright fuchsias grow 45–90 cm (18–36") tall. They can be used in mixed planters, beds and borders. The pendulous fuchsias grow 15–60 cm (6–24") tall. They are most often used in hanging baskets but make attractive additions to planters and rock gardens where the flowers dangle from the flexible branches.

When deadheading fuchsias, pluck the swollen seedpods from behind the fading petals or the seeds will ripen and rob the plant of energy necessary for flower production.

Fuchsias are perennials that are grown as annuals. To store fuchsias over winter, cut back the plants to 15 cm (6") stumps after the first light frost and place them in a dark, cold, but not freezing, location. Water just enough to keep the soil barely moist and do not feed. In mid-spring, re-pot the naked stumps, set them near a bright window and fertilize them lightly. You can set your overwintered plants outdoors the following spring after all danger of frost has passed.

RECOMMENDED

F. x *hybrida.* There are dozens of cultivars; the following are just a few examples. **'Deep Purple'** has purple petals and white sepals. **'Snowburner'** has white petals and pink sepals. **'Swingtime'** has white petals with pink bases and pink sepals. This plant grows 30–60 cm (12–24") tall and spreads about 15 cm (6"). It can be grown in a hanging basket or as a relaxed upright plant in beds and borders. **'Winston Churchill'** has purple petals and pink sepals. The plant grows 20–75 cm (8–30") tall, with an equal spread. The plant is quite upright in form but is often grown in hanging baskets. Many of the available hybrids cannot be started from seed.

PROBLEMS & PESTS

Common insect pests are aphids, spider mites and whiteflies. Diseases such as crown rot, root rot and rust can be avoided with good air circulation and drainage.

Some gardeners who have kept fuchsias over several years have trained the plants to adopt a tree form.

Gazania
Gazania

Height: usually 15–20 cm (6–8"); may reach 30–45 cm (12–18")
Spread: 20–30 cm (8–12") **Flower colour:** red, orange, yellow, pink or cream

My first year of gardening I was captivated by the sight of Gazania. I was then disappointed to discover that the flowers stayed closed on dull days. With the introduction of cultivars like the 'Daybreak' series that stay open longer, few other flowers can rival Gazania for adding vivid oranges, reds and yellows to the garden.

PLANTING

Seeding: Indoors in late winter; direct sow after last frost.

Planting out: After last frost.

Spacing: 15–25 cm (6–10").

GROWING

Gazania grows best in **full sun** but tolerates partial shade. The soil should be of **poor to average fertility, sandy** and **well drained**. This plant grows best in hot weather over 27° C (80° F).

TIPS

Low-growing Gazania makes an excellent groundcover and is also useful on exposed slopes, in mixed containers and for edging flowerbeds.

RECOMMENDED

G. rigens forms a low basal rosette of lobed foliage. Large daisy-like flowers with pointed petals are borne on strong stems above the plant. The flowers often have a contrasting stripe down the centre, or a spot at the base, of each petal. These flowers tend to close on gloomy days and in low-light situations. The species is rarely grown, but several hybrid cultivars are available. **'Daybreak'** series bears flowers in many colours, often with a contrasting stripe down the centre of each petal. These flowers will stay open on dull days, but close on rainy or very dark days. **'Mini-Star'** series has compact plants and flowers in many colours with a contrasting dot at the base of each petal. **'Sundance'** bears flowers in reds and yellows with dark, contrasting stripes down the centres of the petals.

PROBLEMS & PESTS

Over-watering is the likely cause of any problems encountered by Gazania.

Geranium
Pelargonium

Height: 20–60 cm (8–24") **Spread:** 15–120 cm (6–48")
Flower colour: red, pink, violet, orange, salmon, white or purple

*T*ough, predictable, sun-loving and drought-resistant, geraniums have earned their place as favourites in the annual garden. The flowers and foliage have a strong impact, making them good focal plants in mixed planters and containers. Add more delicate plants such as Sweet Alyssum, Bacopa and Dusty Miller to the planter for balance. Ivy-leaved Geranium is delicate and airy and is wonderful alone, or with other trailing annuals, in hanging baskets.

PLANTING

Seeding: Indoors in early winter; direct sow in spring.

Planting out: After last frost.

Spacing: Zonal Geranium, about 30 cm (12"); Ivy-leaved Geranium, 60–90 cm (24–36").

GROWING

Geraniums prefer **full sun** but will tolerate **partial shade**, although they may not bloom as profusely. The soil should be **fertile** and **well drained**.

Geraniums are slow to grow from seed, so purchasing plants may prove easier. However, if you would like to try starting your own from seed, start them indoors in early winter and cover them with clear plastic to maintain humidity until they germinate. Once the seedlings have three or four leaves, transplant them into individual 8–10 cm

P. zonale

(3–4") pots. Keep them in bright locations because they need lots of light to maintain compact shape.

Deadheading is essential to keep geraniums blooming and looking neat. The flowerheads are attached to long stems that break off easily where they attach to the plant. Some gardeners prefer to snip off just the flowering end in order to avoid potentially damaging the stem.

P. pelatum

TIPS

Geraniums are very popular annual plants. Use Zonal Geranium in beds, borders and containers. Ivy-leaved Geranium is most often used in hanging baskets and containers to take advantage of its trailing habit, but it is also interesting when used as a bedding plant where it forms a bushy, spreading groundcover.

Geraniums are perennials that are treated as annuals. They can be kept indoors over winter in a bright room.

RECOMMENDED

The following species and varieties are some of the easier ones to start from seed. Many popular varieties can be propagated only from cuttings and must be purchased as plants.

P. peltatum (Ivy-leaved Geranium) grows up to 30 cm (12") tall and up to 4' (1.2 m) wide. Many colours are available. Plants in the **'Summer Showers'** series can take four or more months to flower from seed. The **'Tornado'** series is very good for

P. zonale

hanging baskets and containers. The plants are quite compact, and the flowers are either lilac or white.

P. zonale (Zonal Geranium) grows up to 60 cm (24") tall and 30 cm (12") wide. Dwarf varieties grow up to 20 cm (8") tall and 15 cm (6") wide. The flowers are red, pink, purple, orange or white. **'Orbit'** series has attractive early-blooming, compact plants. The seed is often sold in a mixed packet, but some individual colours are available. **'Pinto'** series is available in all colours, and seed is generally sold by the colour so you don't have to purchase a mixed packet and hope you like the colours you get.

PROBLEMS & PESTS

Aphids will flock to overfertilized plants, but they can usually be washed off before they do much damage. Leaf spot and blight may bother geraniums growing in cool, moist soil.

Edema is an unusual condition to which geraniums are susceptible. This disease occurs when a plant is overwatered and the leaf cells burst. A warty surface develops on the leaves. There is no cure, although it can be avoided through careful watering and by removing any damaged leaves as the plant grows. The condition is more common in Ivy-leaved Geranium.

P. zonale

Ivy-leaved Geranium is one of the most beautiful plants to include in a mixed hanging basket.

P. zonale

Globe Amaranth

Gomphrena

Height: 15–75 cm (6–30") **Spread:** 15–30 cm (6–12")
Flower colour: purple, pink, white or sometimes red

*G*lobe Amaranth is a truly happy-looking plant. With clover-like flowerheads in colours straight from a candy factory, Globe Amaranth injects merriness into the annual garden. This plant was long grown as an everlasting, and the flowerheads can be used to make a rainbow-coloured garland.

Globe Amaranth flowers are popular for cutting and drying because they keep their colour and form well when dried.

PLANTING

Seeding: Indoors in late winter.

Planting out: After last frost.

Spacing: 25 cm (10").

GROWING

Globe Amaranth prefers **full sun**. The soil should be of **average fertility** and **well drained**. This plant likes hot weather.

Seeds will germinate more quickly if soaked for two to four days before sowing. They need warm soil above 21° C (70° F) to sprout.

TIPS

Use Globe Amaranth in an informal or cottage garden. These plants are often underused because they don't start flowering until later in summer than many other annuals. Don't overlook them—they are worth the wait and provide colour from mid-summer until the first frost.

RECOMMENDED

G. globosa forms a rounded, bushy plant 30–60 cm (12–24") tall that is dotted with papery, clover-like flowers. **'Buddy'** has more compact plants, 15–30 cm (6–12") tall, with deep purple flowers. **'Lavender Lady'** grows into a large plant, up to 60 cm (24") tall, and bears lavender purple flowers.

G. **'Strawberry Fields'** is a hybrid with bright orange-red flowers. It grows about 75 cm (30") tall and spreads about half as much.

PROBLEMS & PESTS

Globe Amaranth is susceptible to some fungal diseases, such as grey mould and leaf spot.

Pick the flowers before they are completely open and dry them upside down in a cool, dry location.

Godetia
Clarkia, Satin Flower
Clarkia (Godetia)

Height: 30–90 cm (12–36") **Spread:** 25–30 cm (10–12")
Flower colour: pink, red- to purple-toned, or white; some bicoloured

*T*he first time I saw godetia in a garden I was bewitched. The flowers in pink, salmon, purple, rose and scarlet are beautifully tropical, yet this is a North American native; in fact, its alternate genus name, *Clarkia*, is from Captain William Clark of the Lewis and Clark expeditions. Buy a packet of seeds, spread them around and watch as these beauties quickly fill your garden.

PLANTING
Seeding: Direct sow in spring or late summer.

Spacing: 15 cm (6").

GROWING
Godetias will grow equally well in **full sun** or **light shade**. The soil should be **well drained, light, sandy** and of **poor or average fertility.** These plants don't like to be over-watered, so be sure to let them dry out between waterings. They do well in cool weather.

Starting seeds indoors is not recommended. Direct sow seeds in spring for summer blooms and in mid- to late summer for fall blooms. Seed plants where you want them to grow, because they are difficult to transplant. Thin seedlings to about 15 cm (6") apart.

TIPS
Godetias are useful in beds, borders, containers and rock gardens. The flowers can be used for fresh arrangements.

RECOMMENDED
C. amoena (*Godetia amoena, G. grandiflora*) (Godetia, Satin Flower) is a bushy, upright plant. It grows up to 75 cm (30") tall, spreads 30 cm (12") and bears clusters of ruffled, cup-shaped flowers in shades of pink, red, white and purple. **'Satin'** series has compact plants that grow 20–30 cm (8–12") tall. The single flowers come in many colours, including some bicolours.

'Satin' series

C. unguiculata (C. elegans) (Clarkia, Rocky Mountain Garland Flower) is a tall, branching plant that grows 30–90 cm (12–36") tall and spreads up to 25 cm (10"). Its small ruffled flowers can be pink, purple, red or white. **'Apple Blossom'** bears double apricot-pink flowers. **'Royal Bouquet'** bears very ruffled double flowers in pink, red or light purple.

PROBLEMS & PESTS
Root rot can occur in poorly drained soil.

This plant produces gorgeous showy flowers despite its preference for poor soil.

Heliotrope
Cherry Pie Plant
Heliotropium

Height: 20–60 cm (8–24") **Spread:** 30–60 cm (12–24")
Flower colour: purple, occasionally white

For years I waited to be bowled over by the scent of Heliotrope. It finally happened when I went for a stroll through the Scented Garden at the Royal Botanical Gardens in Hamilton, Ontario. It was a very hot, still day, and a mass planting of Heliotrope gave off a deep, satisfying aroma like a warm cherry pie. Along with the fragrance, there is much to admire about Heliotrope. The foliage is always an impeccable, neatly creased dark green. The clusters of flowers are deep purple. Heliotrope seems to ward off insect attack and looks fresh in the ground or in containers all summer long.

PLANTING
Seeding: Indoors in mid-winter.

Planting out: Once soil has warmed.

Spacing: 30–45 cm (12–18").

GROWING
Heliotrope grows best in **full sun**. The soil should be **fertile,** rich in **organic** matter, **moist** and **well drained.**

TIPS
Heliotrope is ideal for growing in containers or in beds near windows and patios where the wonderful scent of the flowers can be enjoyed.

'Marine'

These plants can be pinched and shaped. Create a tree form by pinching off the lower branches as the plant grows until it reaches the height you desire; then pinch the top to encourage the plant to bush out. A shorter, bushy form is most popular. Pinch all the tips that develop to encourage the plant to bush out at ground level.

Heliotrope can be grown indoors as a houseplant in a sunny window. The plants may survive for years if kept outdoors all summer and indoors all winter in a cool, bright room.

RECOMMENDED

H. arborescens is a low, bushy shrub that is treated like an annual. It grows 45–60 cm (18–24") tall, with an equal spread. Large clusters

Plants that are a little underwatered tend to have a stronger scent.

of scented, purple flowers are produced all summer. Some new cultivars are not as strongly scented as the species. **'Blue Wonder,'** however, is a compact plant that was developed to have heavily scented flowers. Plants grow up to 40 cm (16") tall with dark purple flowers. **'Dwarf Marine'** ('Mini Marine') is a compact, bushy plant with fragrant, purple flowers. It grows 20–30 cm (8–12") tall and is a good winter houseplant. **'Marine'** has violet-blue flowers and grows to be about 45 cm (18") tall.

PROBLEMS & PESTS
Aphids and whiteflies can be problems.

These old-fashioned flowers may have been popular in your grandmother's garden. Their recent comeback is no surprise considering their attractive foliage, flowers and scent.

Hollyhock

Alcea

Height: 1.5–2.5 m (5–8') **Spread:** 60 cm (24")
Flower colour: yellow, white, apricot, pink, red, purple or reddish black

*H*ollyhocks, especially the single ones, are sentimental favourites in the garden, even though
their foliage is disfigured beyond recognition by
Hollyhock rust by summer's end. The sight of them
braced up against a simple picket fence is endearing. Plant
them with other tall annuals such as sunflowers, snapdragons and Black-eyed Susan for a display that stands
out at the back of the border.

*The powdered roots of plants in
the mallow family, to which
Hollyhock belongs, were once
used to make a soft lozenge for
sore throats. Though popular
around the campfire, marsh-
mallows no longer contain
the throat soothing properties
they originally did.*

PLANTING

Seeding: Start indoors in early winter.

Planting out: After last frost.

Spacing: 45–60 cm (18–24") apart.

GROWING

Hollyhocks prefer **full sun** but will tolerate partial shade. The soil should be **average to rich** and **well drained.**

TIPS

Because they are so tall, Hollyhocks look best at the back of the border or in the centre of an island bed. In a windy location this plant will need to be staked. Plant it against a fence or wall for support.

If the main stem is pinched out early in the season, Hollyhocks will be shorter and bushier with smaller flower spikes. These shorter stems are less likely to be broken by wind and can be left unstaked.

Old-fashioned types typically have single flowers and grow much taller than newer hybrids but are more disease resistant.

Plant Hollyhocks in a different part of the garden each year to keep Hollyhock rust at bay.

Hollyhock was originally grown as a food plant. The leaves were added to salads.

RECOMMENDED

A. rosea forms a rosette of basal leaves; the tall flowering stalk bears ruffled single or double blooms. **'Chater's Double'** bears double flowers in

a wide range of colours. **'Nigra'** bears reddish-black single flowers with yellow centres. **'Summer Carnival'** bears double flowers in yellows and reds. It blooms in early summer and produces flowers lower on the stem than the other cultivars.

PROBLEMS & PESTS

Hollyhock rust is the biggest problem. Hollyhocks are also susceptible to bacterial and fungal leaf spot. Slugs and cutworms occasionally attack young growth. Sometimes mallow flea beetles, aphids or Japanese beetles cause trouble.

'Nigra'

'Chater's Double'

Impatiens
Impatiens

Height: 15–90 cm (6–36") **Spread:** 30–60 cm (12–24")
Flower colour: shades of purple, red, pink, orange, white or bicoloured

*I*t's no wonder impatiens are the number one annual plants for shady spots. Busy Lizzie is the high-wattage darling of the shade garden, delivering masses of flowers in shades of pink, rose, salmon, mauve, red and white to the gloomy real estate under shade trees. New Guinea Impatiens heats up the garden with flowers in hot red, orange and pink and variegated foliage. Balsam Impatiens is an old-fashioned favourite that has recently experienced a revival of interest with the introduction of several new varieties.

PLANTING

Seeding: Indoors in mid-winter; Balsam Impatiens indoors in late winter.

Planting out: Once soil has warmed.

Spacing: 30–45 cm (12–18").

GROWING

All impatiens will do best in **partial shade** but will tolerate full shade or, if kept moist, full sun. New Guinea Impatiens and Balsam Impatiens are best adapted to sunny locations. The soil should be **fertile, humus-rich, moist** and **well drained**.

When seeding, don't cover seeds—they germinate best when exposed to light.

TIPS

Busy Lizzie is best known for its ability to grow and flower profusely in even the deepest shade. Mass plant in beds under trees, along shady fences or walls, in porch planters or hanging baskets.

New Guinea Impatiens is almost shrubby in form and is popular in patio planters, beds and borders. It grows well in full sun and may not flower as profusely in deep shade. This plant is grown as much for its variegated leaves as for its flowers.

I. New Guinea Group (above and below)

I. walleriana (above), 'Victoria Rose' (below)

Balsam Impatiens was a popular garden plant in the Victorian era and is experiencing a comeback in popularity. This plant's habit is more upright than that of the other two impatiens, and it is attractive when grouped in beds and borders.

RECOMMENDED

New impatiens varieties are introduced every year, expanding the selection of size, form and colour. The following are a few that are popular year after year.

I. balsamina (Balsam Impatiens) grows 30–90 cm (12–36") tall and up to 45 cm (18") wide. The flowers come in shades of purple, red, pink or white. There are several double-flowered cultivars, such as **'Camellia-flowered,'** with double flowers in pink, red or white on plants up to 60 cm (24") tall; **'Tom Thumb'** with

double pink, red, purple or white flowers on compact plants to 30 cm (12") tall; or **'Topknot'** with large, double flowers held above the foliage on plants 30 cm (12") tall.

I. New Guinea Group (New Guinea Impatiens) grows 30–60 cm (12–24") tall and 30 cm (12") wide or wider. The flowers come in shades of red, orange, pink, purple or white. The foliage is often variegated with a yellow stripe down the centre of each leaf. **'Tango'** is the most common variety to grow from seed. The compact plants grow 30–45 cm (12–18") tall and wide and have orange flowers.

I. walleriana (Busy Lizzie) grows 15–45 cm (6–18") tall and up to 60 cm (24") wide. These flowers come in shades of red, orange, pink, purple, white or bicoloured. **'Elfin'** series is a common group of cultivars. The flowers are available in many shades, including bicolours. The compact plants grow about 30 cm (12") tall, but they may spread more. **'Mosaic'** has uniquely coloured flowers. The margins and most of the petals are speckled in a darker shade of the petal colour. **'Tempo'** has a wide range of colours, including bicolours, and flowers with contrasting margins on the petals. **'Victoria Rose'** is an award-winning cultivar, with its deep pink, double or semi-double flowers.

The name Impatiens *refers to the impatient nature of the seedpods. When ripe, the seedpods burst open with the slightest touch and scatter their seeds.*

I. walleriana

Licorice Plant

Helichrysum

Height: 50 cm (20") **Spread:** about 90 cm (36"); sometimes up to 1.8 m (6')
Flower colour: yellow-white; grown for foliage

*T*he introduction of more annuals with lime green foliage or flowers is sharpening the design skills of gardeners. 'Limelight' makes for provocative pairings in containers. It cools down a hot colour scheme and adds dynamic tension to plantings containing dark-coloured specimens such as verbena or the perennial coral bells.

PLANTING
Seeding: Not recommended.

Planting out: After last frost.

Spacing: About 75 cm (30").

GROWING

Licorice Plant prefers **full sun**. The soil should be of **poor to average fertility, neutral or alkaline** and **well drained**. Licorice Plant will wilt if the soil dries out but revives quickly once watered.

It is easy to start more plants from cuttings in fall, giving you a supply of new plants for the following spring. Once they have rooted, keep the young plants in a cool, bright room for winter.

TIPS

Licorice Plant is a perennial that is grown as an annual. It is grown for its foliage, not its flowers. Include it in your hanging baskets and container plantings, and the trailing growth will quickly fill in and provide a soft silvery backdrop for the colourful flowers of other plants. Licorice Plant can also be used as an annual groundcover or as an edger in beds and borders. Licorice Plant will cascade down in a silvery wave over the rocks in rock gardens and along the tops of retaining walls.

'Silver'

This plant is a good indicator plant for hanging baskets. When you see Licorice Plant wilting, it is time to get out the hose or watering can.

RECOMMENDED

H. petiolare is a trailing plant with fuzzy grey-green leaves. The cultivars are more common than the species. **'Limelight'** has bright lime green leaves that need protection from direct sunlight to maintain their colour. It is less common, though well worth hunting for (photo on opposite page). **'Silver'** is a common cultivar. The grey-green leaves are covered in a silvery-white down. **'Variegatum,'** a less common cultivar, has grey-green leaves that are dappled or margined in silvery cream.

PROBLEMS & PESTS

Powdery mildew can be an occasional problem, though you might not see it because the leaves are already soft and white.

Livingstone Daisy
Ice Plant
Dorotheanthus (Mesembryanthemum)

Height: 15 cm (6") **Spread:** 30 cm (12")
Flower colour: crimson, orange, rose, yellow, pink, white or bicoloured

*I*n dry places, such as exposed slopes, Livingstone Daisy forms a stunning groundcover. The large, colourful flowers are held above the fleshy foliage on which tiny, unusual crystals form. Livingstone Daisy doesn't mind heat, but it fades during humid summer weather. In Ontario it is at its best in spring and early summer and then again in late summer and fall.

PLANTING

Seeding: Indoors in late winter; direct sow in spring.

Planting out: After last frost.

Spacing: 30 cm (12").

GROWING

Livingstone Daisy likes to grow in **full sun**. The soil should be **sandy** and **well drained**, with **poor to average fertility**.

TIPS

Brightly flowered and low-growing, Livingstone Daisy can be used to edge borders, on dry slopes, in rock gardens or in mixed containers. It can also be used between the stones or around the edges of a paved patio. The flowers close on cloudy days.

RECOMMENDED

D. bellidiformis (M. criniflorum) is a low-growing, spreading plant. It grows up to 15 cm (6") tall, spreads up to 30 cm (12") and bears brightly coloured, daisy-like flowers. **'Lunette'** ('Yellow Ice') bears bright yellow flowers with red centres. **'Magic Carpet'** series has flowers in shades of purple, pink, white, yellow or orange. The petal bases are often lighter than the tips.

PROBLEMS & PESTS

Slugs, snails and aphids may be troublesome.

These plants are also known as 'ice plants' because of the tiny crystals that form on the leaves.

Lobelia
Edging Lobelia
Lobelia

Height: 10–25 cm (4–10") **Spread:** 15 cm (6") or wider
Flower colour: purple, blue, pink, white or red

*L*obelia adds rich jewel tones to the garden. It looks sumptuous in hanging baskets where the blues and purples form dense domes of colour. Gardeners who have tried Lobelia and been disappointed by its lax habit and intolerance of heat should try the 'Regatta' series. This trailing cultivar bears flowers of many colours, has dense growth and is forgiving of heat and drought.

PLANTING

Seeding: Indoors in mid-winter.

Planting out: After last frost.

Spacing: 15 cm (6").

GROWING

Lobelia grows well in **full sun** or **partial shade**. The soil should be **fertile,** high in **organic** matter, **moist** and **fairly well drained**. Lobelia likes cool summer nights.

Lobelia seedlings are prone to damping off. See the 'Starting Annuals from Seed' section in the introduction for information on proper propagation techniques to help avoid damping off.

TIPS

Use Lobelia along the edges of beds and borders, on rock walls, in rock gardens, mixed containers or hanging baskets.

Trim Lobelia back after the first wave of flowers. It will stop blooming in the hottest part of summer but will usually revive in fall.

RECOMMENDED

L. erinus may be rounded and bushy or low and trailing. It grows 10–25 cm (4–10") tall, with an equal spread, and bears flowers in shades of blue, purple, red, pink or white. **'Cascade'** series is a trailing form with flowers in many shades. **'Crystal Palace'** is a compact plant that rarely achieves 10 cm (4") in height. This cultivar has dark green foliage and dark blue flowers. **'Regatta'** series is a trailing cultivar that is more heat tolerant and blooms longer than the other cultivars. **'Riviera'** series has flowers in shades of blue and purple on bushy plants. **'Sapphire'** has white-centered blue flowers on trailing plants.

PROBLEMS & PESTS

Rust, leaf spot and slugs may be troublesome.

'Sapphire' (above),
'Cascade' series (below)

Love-in-a-Mist
Devil-in-a-Bush
Nigella

Height: 40–60 cm (16–24") **Spread:** 20–30 cm (8–12")
Flower colour: blue, white, pink or purple

*L*ove-in-a-mist has gauzy, fern-like foliage and starry flowers of clear blue. It contrasts beautifully with plants of rigid form such as irises. In addition to lifting the spirits of heavy-leaved neighbours, Love-in-a-mist produces attractive seedheads after flowering.

PLANTING

Seeding: Indoors in peat pots or pellets in late winter; direct sow in early spring.

Planting out: Mid-spring.

Spacing: 25–40 cm (10–15").

GROWING

Love-in-a-mist prefers to grow in **full sun**. The soil should be of **average fertility, light** and **well drained**.

Direct sow seeds at two-week intervals all spring to prolong the blooming period. This plant resents having its roots disturbed. Seeds started indoors should be planted in peat pots or pellets to avoid damaging the roots when the plant is transplanted into the garden.

Love-in-a-mist has a tendency to self-sow and may show up in unexpected spots in your garden for years to come.

TIPS

This attractive, airy plant is often used in mixed beds and borders where the flowers appear to be floating over the delicate foliage. The blooming may slow down and the plants may die back if the weather gets too hot for them during the summer.

The stems of this plant can be a bit floppy and may benefit from being staked with twiggy branches. Poke the branches in around the plants while they are young, and the plants will grow up between the twigs.

RECOMMENDED

N. damascena forms a loose mound of finely divided foliage. It grows 45–60 cm (18–24") tall and spreads about half this much. The light blue flowers darken as they mature. '**Miss Jekyll**' series bears semi-double flowers in rose pink or sky blue or a deep cornflower blue that pairs especially well with golden yellow coreopsis. The plants grow to about 45 cm (18") in height. '**Mulberry Rose**' bears light pink flowers that mature to dark pink. '**Persian Jewel**' series is one of the most common cultivars. Plants in this series usually grow to 40 cm (16") tall and have flowers in many colours.

Both the flowers and the seedpods are popular for flower arrangements. The flowers are long lasting in fresh arrangements and the pods can be dried once they are ripe and used in dried arrangements.

Madagascar Periwinkle
Catharanthus

Height: 15–60 cm (6–24") **Spread:** usually equal to or greater than height
Flower colour: red, rose, pink, mauve or white; often with contrasting centres

*I*f planted close together, Madagascar Periwinkle plants will form a very handsome small hedge. These are sturdy plants with glossy leaves and showy white, pink or rose-coloured flowers with contrasting centres. Madagascar Periwinkle is a forgiving annual, tolerant of dry spells, searing sun and city pollution. It exhibits grace under all sorts of pressure.

PLANTING
Seeding: Indoors in mid-winter.

Planting out: After last frost.

Spacing: 20–45 cm (8–18").

GROWING

Madagascar Periwinkle prefers **full sun** but tolerates partial shade. **Any soil** is fine. This plant will tolerate pollution and drought but prefers to be watered regularly, and it doesn't like to be too wet or too cold.

Keep seedlings warm and take care not to overwater them. The soil temperature should be 13–18° C (55–64° F) for seeds to germinate.

TIPS

Madagascar Periwinkle will do well in the sunniest, warmest part of the garden. Plant in a bed along an exposed driveway or against the south-facing wall of the house. It can also be used in hanging baskets, planters and as a temporary groundcover.

This plant is a perennial that is grown as an annual. In a bright room, it can be grown as a houseplant.

RECOMMENDED

C. roseus forms a mound of strong stems. The plants grow 30–60 cm (12–24") tall, with an equal spread, and the flowers are pink, red or white, often with contrasting centres. **'Apricot Delight'** bears pale apricot flowers with bright raspberry red centres. **'Cooler'** series has light coloured flowers with darker, contrasting centres. **'Pacifica'** has flowers in various colours on compact plants.

PROBLEMS & PESTS

Slugs can be troublesome. Most rot and fungus-related problems can be avoided by not overwatering the plants.

One of the best annuals to use in front of homes on busy streets, Madagascar Periwinkle will bloom happily despite exposure to exhaust fumes and dust.

Mallow

Lavatera

Height: 50–300 cm (20–120") **Spread:** 45–150 cm (18–60")
Flower colour: rose, pink, salmon or white

*M*allows are indispensable. Use these plants to fill in gaps in a new perennial garden—they are big, bushy, and lavishly covered in cup-shaped flowers all summer. 'Silver Cup' is a very pretty satin pink, gorgeous as it unrolls its cup-shaped flowers. I saw it in a planting with annual salvias, godetia and poppies, and the whole effect was fresh and sweet.

PLANTING

Seeding: Indoors in late winter; direct sow in spring.

Planting out: After last frost.

Spacing: 45–60 cm (18–24").

GROWING

Mallows prefer **full sun**. The soil should be of **average fertility, light** and **well drained**. These plants like cool, moist weather. Select a site where the plants will be protected from wind exposure.

These plants resent having their roots disturbed when they are transplanted and tend to do better when planted directly in the garden. If you choose to start seeds indoors, use peat pots.

TIPS

Mallow plants can be used as colourful backdrops behind smaller plants in a bed or border. They can

'Mont Blanc' (above), 'Silver Cup' (below)

also be used as temporary hedges along a property line or driveway. The blooms make attractive cut flowers and are edible.

Mallows grow to be fairly large and shrubby. Stake tall varieties to keep them from falling over in summer rain.

RECOMMENDED

L. arborea (Tree Mallow) is a large plant, capable of growing 3 m (10') tall and spreading 1.5 m (5'). The funnel-shaped flowers are pinkish purple. The lifespan of this plant is undetermined; typically grown as an annual, it can sometimes be treated as a biennial or perennial. The cultivar **'Variegata'** has cream-mottled leaves.

L. cachemiriana has light pink flowers. It can grow up to 2.5 m (8') tall and is usually half as wide. It is native to Kashmir.

L. cachemiriana (above), 'Silver Cup' (below)

L. trimestris is large and bushy, growing up to 120 cm (48") tall and spreading 45–60 cm (18–24"). This plant bears red, pink or white, funnel-shaped flowers. **'Beauty'** series has plants in a variety of colours. **'Mont Blanc'** bears white flowers on compact plants that grow to about 50 cm (20") tall. **'Silver Cup'** has cup-shaped light pink flowers with dark pink veins.

Though there are only 25 species of Lavatera, *they are a diverse group containing annuals, biennials, perennials and shrubs.*

PROBLEMS & PESTS
Plant in well-drained soil to avoid root rot. Destroy any rust-infected plants.

Marigold

Tagetes

Height: 15–90 cm (6–36") tall **Spread:** 30–45 cm (12–18")
Flower colour: yellow, red, orange or cream and bicolours

*I*t seems few plants stand up as well as marigolds in the hot, humid Ontario summers. From the large, exotic, ruffled flowers of African Marigold to the tiny flowers on the low growing Signet Marigold, the warm colours of marigold flowers and the fresh scent of the foliage add a festive touch to the garden.

When using marigolds as cut flowers, remove the lower leaves to take away some of the pungent scent.

PLANTING

Seeding: Start indoors in spring or earlier.

Planting out: Once soil has warmed.

Spacing: Dwarf marigolds, 15 cm (6"); tall marigolds, 30 cm (12").

GROWING

Marigolds grow best in **full sun**. The soil should be of **average fertility** and **well drained**. These plants are drought tolerant.

TIPS

Mass planted or mixed with other plants, marigolds make a vibrant addition to beds, borders and container gardens. These plants will thrive in the hottest, driest parts of your garden.

T. erecta (above), *T. patula* (below)

Remove spent blooms to encourage more flowers and to keep plants tidy.

RECOMMENDED

T. erecta (African Marigold; American Marigold; Aztec Marigold) is 50–90 cm (20–36") tall, with huge flowers. **'Cracker Jack'** series bears large, double flowers in bright shades of orange and yellow on tall plants that grow up to 90 cm (36") tall. **'Inca'** bears double flowers in solid or multi-coloured shades of yellow, gold and orange on compact plants that grow to 45 cm (18") tall. **'Marvel'** is a more compact cultivar, growing only 45 cm (18") tall, but with the large flowers that make this species popular. **'Vanilla'** bears unique, cream-white flowers on compact, odourless plants.

T. patula (French Marigold) is low growing, only 18–25 cm (7–10") tall. **'Bonanza'** series is another popular double-flowered cultivar. Its flowers are red, orange, yellow and bicoloured. **'Janie'** series is a popular double-flowered cultivar. It is an early-blooming, compact plant with red, orange and yellow blooms.

T. tenuifolia (Signet Marigold) has dainty, single flowers that grow on

T. tenuifolia

bushy plants with feathery foliage. **'Gem'** series is commonly available. The compact plants, about 25 cm (10") tall, bear flowers in shades of yellow and orange, and the blooms last all summer.

T. Triploid Hybrids (Triploid Marigolds) have been developed by crossing African Marigold and French Marigold. The resulting plants have the huge flowers of African Marigold and the compact growth of French Marigold. These hybrids are the most heat resistant of all the marigolds. They generally grow about 30 cm (12") tall and spread 30–60 cm (12–24"). **'Nugget'** bears large yellow, red, orange, gold or bicoloured flowers on low, wide-spreading plants.

PROBLEMS & PESTS
Slugs and snails can eat seedlings to the ground.

T. tenuifolia *is used as a culinary or tea herb in some Latin American countries.*

T. erecta *and* T. patula *are often used in vegetable gardens for their reputed insect-repelling abilities.*

T. patula

Mexican Sunflower
Tithonia

Height: 1.2–1.8 m (4–6') **Spread:** 30–60 cm (12–24")
Flower colour: orange, red-orange or yellow-orange

*M*exican Sunflower comes in a most satisfying shade of orange, the velvety texture of the flower petals lending depth to the colour. Despite its powerful colours of orange, red and yellow, Mexican Sunflower harmonizes well with other oranges and yellows in the garden. It is a handsome, bold and big plant that could anchor a border of hot-coloured plants.

Sear ends of cut flowers with a flame. For a hot look along a sunny fence or wall, mix Mexican Sunflower with sunflowers and marigolds.

PLANTING

Seeding: Indoors in early spring; direct sow in spring.

Planting out: Once soil has warmed.

Spacing: 30–60 cm (12–24").

GROWING

Mexican Sunflower grows best in **full sun.** The soil should be of **average to poor fertility** and **well drained.** Cover seeds lightly because they germinate more evenly and quickly when exposed to some light. Mexican Sunflower needs little water or care; however, it will bloom more profusely if it is deadheaded regularly.

TIPS

Mexican Sunflower is heat resistant, so it is ideal for growing in a sunny, dry, warm spot such as under the eaves of a south-facing wall. The plants are tall and break easily if exposed to too much wind; grow along a wall or fence to provide shelter and stability. These annuals are coarse in appearance and are well suited to the back of a border where they provide a good backdrop to a bed of shorter plants.

RECOMMENDED

T. rotundifolia is a vigorous, bushy plant. It grows 1–1.8 m (3–6') tall and spreads 30–60 cm (12–24"). Vibrant orange-red flowers are produced from mid- to late summer through to frost. **'Goldfinger'** grows 60–90 cm (24–36") tall and bears large orange flowers. **'Torch'** has bright red-orange flowers. **'Yellow Torch'** has bright yellow flowers.

PROBLEMS & PESTS

This plant is generally resistant to most problems; however, young foliage may suffer slug and snail damage. Aphids can become a real problem if not dealt with immediately.

'Torch'

Million Bells
Calibrachoa
Calibrachoa

Height: 15–30 cm (6–12") **Spread:** up to 60 cm (24")
Flower colour: pink, purple, yellow, orange or white

*M*illion Bells made its debut described as a tiny petunia and has now been given its own botanical name. Just a few plants will fill a container with mounds of colour, overflow from hanging baskets or spread neatly through a flowerbed. The colours are bright but not overwhelming, with several unique shades not found in petunias.

PLANTING

Seeding: Seeds may not be available.

Planting out: After last frost.

Spacing: 15–40 cm (6–15").

GROWING

Million Bells prefers to grow in **full sun**. The soil should be **fertile, moist** and **well drained**. Though it prefers to be watered regularly, Million Bells is fairly drought resistant in cool and warm climates. Million Bells will bloom well into fall; the flowers become hardy as the weather cools and can survive temperatures down to –7° C (20° F).

TIPS

Popular for planters and hanging baskets, Million Bells is also attractive in beds and borders. This plant grows all summer and needs plenty of room to spread or it will overtake other flowers. Pinch the flowers back to keep plants compact. In a hanging basket, it will toll out millions of bell-shaped blooms.

To protect the petals from rain, place hanging baskets under the eaves of the house or porch.

RECOMMENDED

Calibrachoa hybrids represent a new and distinct species developed from petunias and other plants. The **'Million Bells'** series includes **'Trailing Pink'** with rose-pink, yellow-centered flowers; **'Trailing Blue'** with dark blue or purple, yellow-centered flowers and **'Trailing White'** with white, yellow-centered flowers. **'Terracotta'** has reddish-orange flowers, and **'Yellow'** has bright yellow flowers; these two unique colours truly distinguish Million Bells from petunias.

PROBLEMS & PESTS

Wet weather and cloudy days could cause leaf spot and delayed blooming. Watch for slugs and earwigs that like to nibble on the petals.

'Trailing Pink'

'Trailing Pink' and 'Trailing Blue'

Monkey Flower
Mimulus

Height: 15–30 cm (6–12") **Spread:** 30–60 cm (12–24")
Flower colour: bright and pastel shades of orange, yellow,
burgundy, pink, red or cream

*A*ll manner of dots, dashes and splotches decorate the faces of monkey flowers. Put these plants in baskets in semi-shade and enjoy looking for the happy markings on the five-petalled flowers. Everyone should grow a monkey flower plant at least once.

PLANTING
Seeding: Indoors in early spring.

Planting out: Once soil warms after last frost.

Spacing: 25–30 cm (10–12") apart.

GROWING

Monkey flowers prefer **partial or light shade**. Protection from the afternoon sun will prolong the blooming of these plants. The soil should be **fertile, moist** and **humus rich**. Don't allow the soil to dry out. These plants can become scraggly and unattractive in hot sun.

TIPS

Monkey flower plants make an excellent addition to a border near a pond or to a bog garden. In a flowerbed, border or container garden, these plants will need to be watered regularly.

Monkey flowers are perennials that are grown as annuals. The plants can be overwintered indoors in a cool, bright room.

RECOMMENDED

M. x hybridus are upright annuals with spotted flowers. They grow 15–30 cm (6–12") tall and spread 30 cm (12"). **'Calypso'** bears a mixture of flower colours. **'Mystic'** is

'Mystic'

compact and early flowering and offers a wide range of bright flower colours in solids or bicolours.

M. luteus (Yellow Monkey Flower), though not as common as the hybrids, is worth growing for its low, spreading habit and attractive yellow flowers. It grows about 30 cm (12") tall and spreads up to 60 cm (24"). The yellow flowers are sometimes spotted with red or purple.

PROBLEMS & PESTS

Downy or powdery mildew, grey mould, whiteflies, spider mites and aphids can cause occasional problems.

M. luteus

Morning Glory

Ipomoea

Height: 3–4.5 m (10–15') **Spread:** 30–60 cm (12–24")
Flower colour: white, blue, pink or purple and variegated

Morning Glory 'Heavenly Blue' is sublime when its huge blue flowers are backlit by the sun. Even into fall, when just a few flowers are still clinging to the vine, it seems to hold the whole promise of summer in its paper-thin blossoms. The new darling of the *Ipomoea* group is the Sweet Potato Vine. This vigorous cascading plant in lime green and bruised purple can make any gardener look like a genius. It grows with ease and combines brilliantly with many other annuals and perennials.

PLANTING

Seeding: Indoors in early spring; direct sow after last frost.

Planting out: Late spring.

Spacing: 30–45 cm (12–18").

GROWING

Grow morning glories in **full sun**. Any type of soil will do, but a **light, well-drained** soil with **poor fertility** is preferred. Moonflower needs warm weather to bloom.

Soak seeds for 24 hours before sowing. If starting seeds indoors, sow them in individual peat pots.

TIPS

Morning glories can be grown anywhere: fences, walls, trees, trellises and arbours are all possible frames for these plants. As groundcovers, they will grow over any obstacles they encounter. They can also be grown in hanging baskets.

Morning glories must twine around objects in order to climb them. Wide fence posts, walls or other broad objects must have a trellis or some wire or twine attached to them to provide the vines with something to grow on.

If you have a bright sunny window, consider starting a hanging basket of morning glories indoors for a unique winter display. The vines will twine around the hangers and spill over the sides of the pot, providing you with beautiful trumpet flowers, regardless of the weather outside.

I. tricolor (above)

I. alba (above), 'Blackie' (below)

Each flower of a morning glory plant lasts for only one day. The buds form a spiral that slowly unfurls as the day brightens with the rising sun.

RECOMMENDED
I. tricolor has several cultivars, including the popular **'Heavenly Blue,'** which has true sky blue flowers with a white centre.

ALTERNATE SPECIES
I. alba (Moonflower) has sweet-scented white flowers that open only at night. It grows up to 4.5 m (15') tall.

I. batatas (Sweet Potato Vine) is a twining climber that is grown for its attractive foliage rather than its flowers. Often used in planters and hanging baskets, Sweet Potato Vine can be used by itself or mixed with other plants. **'Blackie'** has dark purple (almost black), deeply lobed leaves. **'Terrace Lime'**

Grow Moonflower on a porch or on a trellis near a patio that is used in the evenings, so the sweetly scented flowers can be fully enjoyed. The buds may close on cloudy days, but once evening falls, the huge, white blossoms pour forth their sweet nectar, attracting night-flying moths.

has yellow-green foliage on a fairly compact plant. These cascading plants can also be trained to grow up a trellis. As a bonus, when you pull up your plants at the end of summer you can eat the tubers (sweet potatoes) that form on the roots.

PROBLEMS & PESTS

Morning glories are susceptible to several fungal problems, but they occur only rarely.

Sweet Potato Vine is best recognized by the large lime green, heart-shaped leaves, but it is also available in shades of purple. Unlike the more aggressive members of the family, Sweet Potato Vine doesn't twine or grasp or get carried away. Instead, it drapes politely over the sides of containers or spreads neatly over the soil beneath taller plants.

I. alba (above), 'Terrace Lime' (below)

Nasturtium
Tropaeolum

Height: 30–45 cm (12–18") for dwarf varieties; up to 3 m (10') for trailing varieties
Spread: equal to or a bit wider than height
Flower colour: red, orange, yellow, pink, white or bicoloured

Nasturtiums have endearing foliage. The wobbly rounded leaves look like they were drawn by a child. The flowers are super-charged—school bus yellow and stop sign red. In addition to these qualities, the edible foliage and flowers have a peppery fire. I love nasturtiums wholeheartedly.

PLANTING

Seeding: Indoors in late winter; direct sow in mid-spring.

Planting out: After last frost.

Spacing: 30 cm (12").

GROWING

Nasturtiums prefer **full sun** but will tolerate partial shade. The soil should be of **average to poor fertility, light, moist** and **well drained**. Let the soil drain completely between waterings.

If you start nasturtium seeds indoors, sow them in individual peat pots to avoid disturbing the roots during transplanting.

'Jewel' series

TIPS

Nasturtiums are used in beds, borders, containers and hanging baskets and on sloped banks. The climbing varieties are also used to grow up trellises or over rocks on walls and other places that need concealing. These plants thrive in poor locations, and they make an interesting addition to plantings on hard-to-mow slopes.

RECIPE
POOR MAN'S CAPERS
(PICKLED NASTURTIUM SEEDPODS)

Soak green seeds in a brine made from 500 ml (2 cups) of water and 12 ml (1 tsp.) salt for 24 hours.

Pack small sterilized jars with the seeds, a peeled clove of garlic and 12 ml (1 tsp.) pickling spices.

Heat white wine vinegar to simmering and fill each jar with the vinegar.

Seal with acid-proof lids and let the seeds sit for about a month.

The pickled seeds should be eaten within a week after opening.

Nasturtiums have a place in the vegetable or herb garden. The leaves and flowers are edible and can be added to salads, soups and dips to add a peppery flavour. The unripe seeds can be pickled and used as a substitute for capers.

Some gardeners believe that nasturtiums attract and harbour certain pests, such as whiteflies and aphids, and that they should not be grown near plants that are susceptible to the same problems. Other gardeners believe that nasturtiums are preferred by pest insects and that the pests will flock to them and leave the rest of the garden alone. Still other gardeners claim that these plants, because of the high sulfur levels in the leaves, repel many pests that would otherwise infest the garden. I have yet to notice nasturtium's influence, for better or worse, on the pest populations in my garden.

RECOMMENDED

T. majus has a trailing habit. It has been greatly improved by hybridizing. The foliage of the older varieties tended to hide the flowers, but new varieties hold their flowers (available in a great selection of colours) above the foliage. There are also some new and interesting cultivars with variegated foliage and compact, attractive, mound-forming habits. **'Alaska'** series has white-marbled foliage. **'Jewel'** series has compact plants that grow to 30 cm (12") tall and wide, with double flowers in a mix of deep orange, red or gold. **'Peach Melba'** forms a 30 cm (12") mound. The flowers are pale yellow with a bright orange-red splash at the base of each petal. **'Whirlybird'** is a compact, bushy plant. The single or double flowers in shades of red, pink, yellow or orange do not have spurs.

PROBLEMS & PESTS

The few problems that afflict nasturtiums include aphids, slugs, whiteflies and some viruses.

'Alaska' series

Nicotiana
Flowering Tobacco Plant
Nicotiana

Height: 30–150 cm (12–60") **Spread:** 30 cm (12")
Flower colour: red, pink, green, yellow, white or purple

My favorite nicotiana remains *N. sylvestris*. Even though it is somewhat wild and untamed, I grew it by the front door in my tiny urban front yard. It is a giant of a plant—when the flowers appeared in August they were five feet in the air, and the leaves were big enough to hide a cat. It framed the front door with a fairy-tale quality. But there are many other nicotianas of modest size that have much charm. I particularly like those with white flowers that have pink backs to the petals.

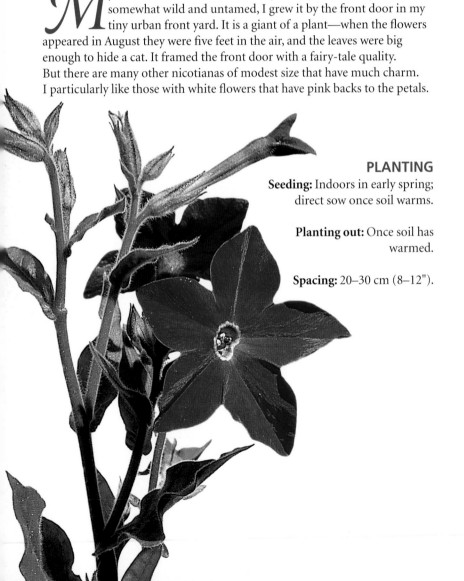

PLANTING

Seeding: Indoors in early spring; direct sow once soil warms.

Planting out: Once soil has warmed.

Spacing: 20–30 cm (8–12").

GROWING

Nicotiana will grow equally well in **full sun** or **light or partial shade**. The soil should be **fertile,** high in **organic** matter, **moist** and **well drained**. The seeds require light for germination, so leave them uncovered.

TIPS

Nicotianas are popular in beds and borders. The dwarf varieties do well in containers. Do not plant nicotianas near tomatoes because as members of the same plant family they share a vulnerability to many of the same diseases. The nicotiana plant may attract and harbour diseases that will hardly affect it but that can kill tomatoes.

N. sylvestris (above), 'Nicki' series (below)

RECOMMENDED

N. alata is an upright plant that grows up to 150 cm (60") tall and has a strong, sweet fragrance. **'Nicki'** series has many coloured, fragrant blooms that open all day. The compact plants grow up to 45 cm (18") tall. **'Merlin'** series has dwarf plants ideal for mixed planters. Its flowers may be red, pink, purple, white or pale green. **'Sensation'** grows up to 75 cm (30") tall and bears red, white or pink flowers that stay open all day.

N. sylvestris grows up to 1.2 m (4') tall and bears white blooms that give off a scent in the evening.

PROBLEMS & PESTS

Tobacco mosaic virus, aphids and downy or powdery mildew may cause occasional problems.

Nicotiana was originally cultivated for the wonderful scent of the flowers. At first, the flowers were only green and opened only in the evening and at night. In attempts to expand the variety of colours and have the flowers open during the day, the popular scent has, in some cases, been lost.

Painted-Tongue
Velvet Flower
Salpiglossis

Height: up to 60 cm (24") **Spread:** 30 cm (12")
Flower colour: red, yellow, orange, pink, purple; often patterned bicolours

*P*hotographs never seem to do these flowers justice. The velvety texture and rich, glossy colours must be seen to be appreciated. The flowers come in a wide range of colours, often with contrasting veins. They look splendid when blended into a planting of Cosmos, Salvia and Phlox and really stand out against a backdrop of Dusty Miller, white-flowered Sweet Alyssum or Baby's Breath.

PLANTING

Seeding: Indoors in late winter; direct sow in spring.

Planting out: After last frost.

Spacing: 30 cm (12").

GROWING

Painted-tongue prefers **full sun.** The soil should be **fertile,** rich in **organic** matter and **well drained.** The seeds are very tiny and shouldn't be covered with soil. They will germinate more evenly if kept in darkness until they sprout—place pots in a dark closet or cover pots with dark plastic or layers of newspaper. Once they start to sprout, the plants can be moved into light.

TIPS

Painted-tongue is useful in the middle or back of beds and borders. It can also be used in large mixed containers. Painted-tongue can become battered in rain and wind. Plant it in warm, sheltered areas of the garden.

RECOMMENDED

S. sinuata is an upright plant related to petunias. **'Blue Peacock'** has blue flowers with yellow throats and dark veins. The plants of the **'Casino'** series, with flowers in a wide range of colours, bloom early and tolerate rain and wind.

PROBLEMS & PESTS

Occasional problems with aphids or root rot are possible.

'Blue Peacock'

The iridescent quality of these flowers causes their colour to change as they turn in a breeze.

Passion Flower
Passiflora

Height: up to 10 m (30')
Flower colour: pale pink petals with blue or purple bands

*P*assion Flower is so intricately beautiful that this plant is worth growing even though flower production is unpredictable. This climber can be grown on a trellis or other support, or it will easily cling with its tendrils onto a rough brick wall. I put it in my southern Ontario garden one year and it overwintered in a sheltered location. However, it needs a long hot summer to produce many flowers, and it did not bloom until November the following year. Overwintering planter specimens in a bright room indoors may be more successful.

PLANTING

Seeding: Not recommended.

Planting out: Several weeks after the last frost.

GROWING

Grow Passion Flower in **full sun** or **partial shade**. This plant prefers **well-drained, fertile** and **moist** soil. Keep this plant sheltered from wind and cold.

Germination is erratic and propagation is generally easier from cuttings, but for gardeners who like a challenge, it is possible to propagate Passion Flower from seed. Place the seed tray in full sun because the seeds need light to germinate. Keep the soil moist and at about 15° C (59° F).

TIPS

Passion Flower is a popular addition to mixed containers and makes an unusual focal point near a door or other entryway. This plant is actually a fast-growing woody climber that is grown as an annual.

Many garden centres now sell small Passion Flower plants in spring which quickly climb trellises and other supports over summer. They can be pulled up at the end of summer or cut back and brought inside to enjoy in a bright room over winter.

The small round fruits are edible, but not very tasty.

RECOMMENDED

P. caerulea (Blue Passion Flower) bears unusual purple-banded, purple-white flowers all summer. **'Constance Elliott'** bears fragrant white flowers.

PROBLEMS & PESTS

Spider mites, whiteflies, scale and nematodes may cause occasional trouble.

These flowers have been regarded by some as symbols of Christ's passion, with the three stigmas representing the nails and the five anthers the wounds.

Petunia

Petunia

Height: 15–45 cm (6–18") **Spread:** 30–60 cm (12–24") or wider
Flower colour: pink, purple, red, white, yellow or bicoloured

For speedy growth, prolific blooming and ease of care, petunias are hard to beat. Still, gardeners have mixed opinions about petunias. Some gardeners absolutely adore them for their profuse blooms and low-maintenance habit. Other gardeners find the flowers garish and dislike the damage they suffer from rain. The wide range of forms, habits, flower sizes and colours means that there are now petunias for every sunny situation. Even long-time petunia snubbers are beginning to take a second look.

PLANTING

Seeding: Indoors in mid-winter.

Planting out: After last frost.

Spacing: 30–45 cm (12–18").

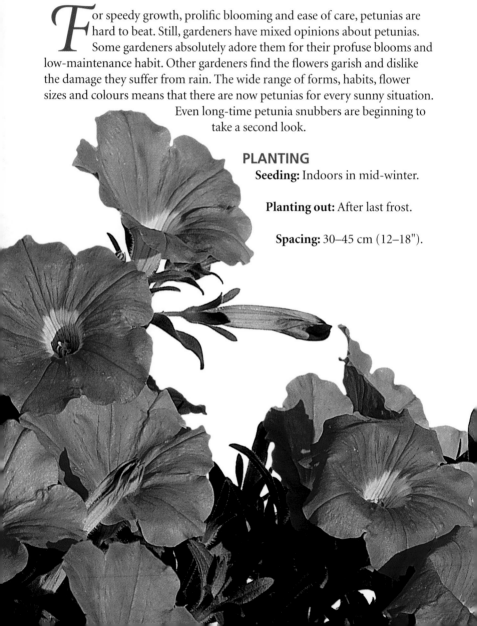

GROWING

Petunias prefer **full sun**. The soil should be of **poor to average fertility, sandy** and **well drained.** When sowing, press seeds into soil surface but don't cover them with soil. Pinch halfway back in mid-summer to keep plants bushy and encourage new growth and flowers.

TIPS

Use petunias in beds, borders, containers and hanging baskets.

RECOMMENDED

P. x *hybrida* is a large group of popular sun-loving annuals that fall into three categories: the grandifloras, the multifloras and the millifloras. The **grandiflora** petunias have the largest flowers—up to 10 cm (4") across. They have the widest variety of colours and forms, but they are the most likely to be damaged by heavy rain.

Multiflora variety

'**Daddy**' series is available in darkly-veined shades of pink and purple. '**Supercascade**' series is available in a wide variety of colours. '**Ultra**' series is available in many colours, including bicolours. This cultivar recovers quite quickly from weather damage.

Compared to the grandifloras, the **multiflora** petunias have smaller blooms (about half the size), bear many more flowers and are more tolerant of adverse weather conditions. '**Carpet**' series is available in a wide variety of colours. '**Wave**' series is available in pink and purple. This plant is popular for hanging baskets and containers. It recovers well from rain damage, blooms a lot and spreads quickly.

The **milliflora** petunias are the newest group. The flowers, about 2.5 cm (1") across, are borne profusely over the whole plant. They tolerate wet weather very well and sometimes self-seed. '**Fantasy**' series is available in shades of red, purple, pink and white, although the pinks tend to be the easiest to find. With this type's growing popularity, more colours will likely become available.

Grandiflora variety (above), Multiflora variety (below)

These petunias are popular in mixed containers and hanging baskets and are also very nice in garden beds, forming neat mounds of foliage and flowers.

PROBLEMS & PESTS

Aphids and fungi may be problems. The fungal problems can be avoided by not wetting the foliage, if possible, and by providing a location with good drainage.

Multiflora variety

Grandiflora variety

Milliflora variety

Phlox
Phlox

Height: 15–45 cm (6–18") **Spread:** 25 cm (10") or wider
Flower colour: purple, pink, red, blue, white or yellow

*P*hlox comes in many appealing colours and fits into a flower border scheme with style. Phlox branches strongly, yet allows the occasional quiet invasion from a harmonious companion plant such as Salvia. Mix Phlox with marigolds, Calendula and Heliotrope for bright colour contrasts.

PLANTING
Seeding: Direct sow in early spring.

Spacing: Up to 20 cm (8").

GROWING

Phlox prefers **full sun**. The soil should be **fertile, moist** and **well drained**. These plants resent being transplanted, and starting them indoors is not recommended. Plant cuttings in moist soil and they will easily root. Germination takes 10–15 days. These plants can be spaced quite close together. Dead-head to promote blooming.

TIPS

Use phlox on rock walls and in beds, borders, containers and rock gardens. To discourage disease, do not over-water and don't let the foliage stay wet at night.

RECOMMENDED

P. drummondii forms a bushy plant that can be upright or spreading and bears clusters of white, purple, pink or red flowers. **'Coral Reef'** bears attractive pastel-coloured flowers. **'Twinkle'** mixed has unusual small, star-shaped flowers on compact plants 20 cm (8") tall. The colours of the petal margins and the centres often contrast with the main petal colour.

PROBLEMS & PESTS

To avoid fungal problems, provide good drainage and don't let water stand on the leaves late in the day. Water the plants in the morning during dry spells and avoid handling wet foliage.

The name phlox is derived from the Greek word meaning 'a flame.'

Poppy
Shirley Poppy, Corn Poppy, Flanders Poppy
Papaver

Height: 60–120 cm (24–48") **Spread:** 30 cm (12")
Flower colour: red, pink, white, purple, yellow or orange

*I*n a garden in Hamilton, Ontario, I once saw a planting of Japanese Iris, Painted Sage and annual poppies. The colours ranged from pink to blue to purple. It was one of the loveliest gardens I have seen and was a strong incentive for me to grow poppies. Poppies add an elusive, poetic beauty to the garden.

PLANTING

Seeding: Direct sow every two weeks in spring.

Spacing: 30 cm (12").

GROWING

Poppies grow best in **full sun**. The soil should be **fertile, sandy** and have lots of **organic** matter mixed in. Good drainage is essential. Do not start seeds indoors because transplanting is often unsuccessful. Mix the tiny seeds with fine sand for even sowing. Deadhead to prolong blooms.

TIPS

Poppies are good in mixed borders where other plants are slow to fill in. Poppies will fill in empty spaces early in the season; then their foliage dies back over summer, leaving room for the other plants. They can also be used in rock gardens, and the cut flowers are popular for fresh arrangements.

The seeds of both Shirley Poppy and Opium Poppy can be used to flavour baked goods such as muffins, breads and bagels.

Be careful when weeding around faded summer plants; you may accidentally pull up late-summer poppy seedlings.

RECOMMENDED

P. rhoeas (Flanders Poppy, Field Poppy) forms a basal rosette of foliage. Its flowers are borne on long stems, held above the foliage. **'Champagne Bubbles'** is strong and bushy with lots of pastel flowers. **'Mother of Pearl'** bears flowers in pastel pinks and purples. **'Shirley'** series has silky cup-shaped petals. The flowers come in many colours and can be single, semi-double or double.

P. somniferum (Opium Poppy) grows up to 120 cm (48") tall. The flowers are red, pink, white or purple. This plant has a mixed reputation. It is the source of several drugs, including codeine, morphine and opium. All parts of the plant can cause stomach upset except for the seeds, which are a

popular culinary additive (poppy seeds). The seeds contain none of the chemicals that make this plant pharmaceutically valuable. The large seed capsules are also dried and used in floral arrangements. Though propagation of the species is restricted in many countries, there are several attractive cultivars that have been developed for ornamental use. **'Danebrog Lace'** originated in the nineteenth century. The single flowers have frilly red petals with a large white patch at the base of each petal. **'Peony Flowered'** has large, frilly double flowers in a variety of colours on plants that grow up to 90 cm (36") tall.

PROBLEMS & PESTS

Poppies rarely have problems, although fungus can occur if the soil is wet and poorly drained.

For cut flowers, seal the cut end of each stem with a flame or boiling water.

Portulaca
Moss Rose
Portulaca

Height: 10–20 cm (4–8") **Spread:** 15–30 cm (6–12") or wider
Flower colour: red, pink, yellow, white, purple or orange

For a brilliant show in the hottest, driest, poorest, most neglected area of the garden, you can't go wrong with Portulaca. My mother grows it in a sandy strip of soil between the house and the driveway. Each year the plants put on a gorgeous show. The stems intermingle and the rose-like flowers of varied, bright colours mix together in harmonious disarray.

PLANTING
Seeding: Indoors in late winter.

Planting out: Once soil has warmed.

Spacing: 30 cm (12").

GROWING
Portulaca requires **full sun**. The soil should be of **poor fertility, sandy** and **well drained**.

To ensure that you will have plants where you want them, seed indoors. If you seed outdoors after the last frost date, tiny seeds may get washed away in rainstorms and the plants will pop up in unexpected places.

Spacing the plants close together is not a problem; in fact, it causes them to intermingle, resulting in well-mixed flower colours.

TIPS

Portulaca is the ideal plant for garden spots that just don't get enough water—under the eaves of the house or in dry, rocky, exposed areas. These plants are ideal for people who like having baskets hanging from the front porch but always forget to water. As long as the location is sunny, the plants will do well with minimal care.

RECOMMENDED

P. grandiflora forms a bushy mound of succulent foliage. It bears delicate, papery, rose-like flowers profusely all summer. **'Cloudbeater'** bears large double flowers in many colours. The flowers stay open all day, even in cloudy weather. **'Sundial'** series has long-lasting double flowers.

PROBLEMS & PESTS

If Portulaca has excellent drainage and as much light as possible, it shouldn't have problems.

These plants will fill a sunny, exposed, narrow strip of soil between any paving and the foundation of a house with bright colours all summer. They require only minimal attention.

Prairie Gentian
Lisianthius
Eustoma

Height: 15–60 cm (6–24") **Spread:** usually half the height
Flower colour: blue, purple, pink, yellow or white

*P*rairie Gentian just begs to be cut and placed in a vase where its beauty can be admired away from all other rivals. It seems too gorgeous to mix in with other garden characters. With blooms in pink, blue, white or purple, it has the charm of roses, tulips and poppies rolled into one flower.

PLANTING

Seeding: Indoors in early winter.

Planting out: Mid-spring.

Spacing: 10–30 cm (4–12"), depending on expected mature size of variety.

GROWING

Prairie Gentian prefers **full sun** but will tolerate light or partial shade. The soil should be of **average fertility** and **well drained**. A **neutral or alkaline** pH is preferred. If your soil is very acidic, then grow the dwarf varieties in pots with an appropriate growing mix instead of struggling to keep these plants healthy in the garden beds.

Seedlings can be quite slow to establish when planted directly in the garden.

TIPS

All varieties of Prairie Gentian look best grouped in flowerbeds or containers. The tallest varieties, with their long-lasting blooms, are popular in cutflower gardens.

RECOMMENDED

E. grandiflora forms a slender upright plant, topped by satiny cup-shaped flowers. **'Echo'** series comes in many colours. This popular tall variety is admired for its double flowers that are excellent for cutflower arrangements. It grows to about 60 cm (24") tall. **'Lisa'** series also comes in many colours. This popular dwarf variety is reputed to bloom from seed one month sooner than other varieties. It grows to about 20 cm (8") tall.

PROBLEMS & PESTS

Generally, this plant is trouble free; however, several diseases, including *Fusarium* wilt, can kill Prairie Gentian. Purchase treated seed from reputable sources and destroy any plants that appear to be diseased before the diseases have a chance to spread to other plants.

A small vase filled with satin-textured Prairie Gentian flowers will add a touch of elegance to any table.

Rocket Larkspur
Annual Delphinium
Consolida (Delphinium)

Height: 30–120 cm (12–48") **Spread:** 15–35 cm (6–14")
Flower colour: blue, purple, pink or white

Gardeners who love blue in the garden should plant Rocket Larkspur. The lovely flower spikes combine so well with other annuals such as Godetia, verbenas and snapdragons. In addition to blue, Rocket Larkspur plants can be found in shades of pink, purple and even grey.

PLANTING

Seeding: Indoors in mid-winter; direct sow in early or mid-spring.

Planting out: Mid-spring.

Spacing: 30 cm (12").

GROWING

Rocket Larkspur will do equally well in **full sun** or **light shade.** The soil should be **fertile,** rich in **organic** matter and **well drained.**

Plant seeds in peat pots to prevent roots from being damaged when the plants are transplanted. Seeds started indoors may benefit from being chilled in the refrigerator for one week prior to sowing. Deadhead to keep these plants blooming well into fall.

These flowers look good at the back of a border and make excellent cut flowers for arrangements.

TIPS

Plant groups of Rocket Larkspur in mixed borders or cottage gardens. The tallest varieties may require staking to stay upright.

Keep the roots of these plants cool and add a light mulch—dried grass clippings or shredded leaves work well. Don't put mulch too close to the base of the plant or the plant may develop crown rot.

RECOMMENDED

C. ajacis *(C. ambigua, D. ajacis)* is an upright plant with feathery foliage that bears spikes of purple, blue, pink or white flowers. **'Dwarf Rocket'** series includes plants that grow between 30–50 cm (12–20") tall and 15–25 cm (6–10")

wide and bloom in many colours. **'Earl Grey'** grows 90–120 cm (36–48") tall and bears flowers in an intriguing colour between slate grey and gun-metal grey. **'Frosted Skies'** grows to 45 cm (18") and bears large semi-double flowers in a breakthrough bicolour of blue and white. **'Giant Imperial'** series also comes in many colours. The plants grow 60–90 cm (24–36") tall and up to 35 cm (14") wide.

PROBLEMS & PESTS
Slugs and snails are potential troublemakers. Powdery mildew and crown or root rot are avoidable if you water thoroughly, but not too often, and make sure the plants have good air circulation.

Salvia
Sage
Salvia

Height: 20–60 cm (8–24") **Spread:** 20–30 cm (8–12")
Flower colour: red, blue, purple, orange, pink or white

*T*he salvias should be part of every annual garden. The attractive and varied forms have something to offer every style of garden. With seed catalogues devoting more attention to the many species, availability is no longer the problem it once was. All the salvias seem spellbinding to insects. In the collection at the University of Guelph Arboretum demonstration gardens, I enjoyed watching a hummingbird moth darting between the reds and blues of a bed of salvias.

PLANTING

Seeding: Indoors in mid-winter; direct sow in spring.

Planting out: After last frost.

Spacing: 25 cm (10").

GROWING

All salvia plants prefer **full sun** but will tolerate light shade. The soil should be **moist** and **well drained** and of **average to rich fertility**, with lots of **organic** matter.

TIPS

Salvias look good grouped in beds and borders and in containers. The flowers are long lasting and make good cut flowers for arrangements.

To keep plants producing flowers, water often and fertilize monthly.

RECOMMENDED

S. farinacea (Blue Sage, Mealy Cup Sage) has bright blue flowers clustered along stems powdered with silver. The plant grows up to 60 cm (24") tall with a spread of 30 cm (12"). The flowers are also available in white. A popular cultivar of *S. farinacea* is **'Victoria,'** with silvery foliage that makes it a beautiful addition to cutflower arrangements.

S. patens (Gentian Sage) bears vivid blue flowers on plants 45–60 cm (18–24") tall. This is a tender perennial grown as an annual. Being tuberous-rooted, it can be lifted and brought inside for the winter the way dahlias are. **'Cambridge Blue'** bears pale blue flowers.

S. splendens (Salvia, Scarlet Sage) grows 30–45 cm (12–18") tall and spreads up to 30 cm (12"). It is known for its spikes of bright red tubular flowers. Recently, cultivars have become available in white, pink, purple and orange. **'Phoenix'** forms neat compact plants with flowers in bright and pastel shades of many colours. **'Salsa'** bears solid

S. splendens

and bicoloured flowers in shades of red, orange, cream and pink. **'Vista'** forms an early-flowering, compact plant with dark blue-green foliage and bright red flowers.

S. viridis (*S. horminium*, Annual Clary Sage) is grown for its colourful bracts, not its flowers. It grows 45–60 cm (18–24") with a spread of 20–30 cm (8–12"). **'Claryssa'** grows 45 cm (18") tall and has bracts in pink, purple, blue or white.

S. viridis has been used externally to relieve sore gums. It has also been used as snuff and to flavour beers and wines.

PROBLEMS & PESTS
Seedlings are prone to damping off. Aphids and a few fungal problems may occur.

S. farinacea

Scabiosa
Pincushion Flower
Scabiosa

Height: 30–90 cm (12–36") **Spread:** up to 40 cm (16")
Flower colour: purple, blue, pink or white

*S*cabiosas are dependable and versatile plants, and the flowers are gaining popularity with flower arrangers. *S. atropurpurea* is a simple, charming plant that blends naturally into a cottage or wildflower garden. *S. stellata* forms unusual orbs of papery seedheads that stand out in dried flower arrangements.

PLANTING
Seeding: Indoors in late winter; direct sow in mid-spring.

Planting out: After last frost.

Spacing: 30–40 cm (12–16").

GROWING

Scabiosas grow best in **full sun**. The soil should be of **average to rich fertility**, **well drained** and be rich in **organic** matter.

TIPS

Scabiosas are useful in beds, borders and mixed containers. The flowers are also popular in fresh arrangements.

The tall stems of *S. atropurpurea* may fall over as the plants mature. Insert twiggy branches into the ground around the plants when they are small to give them support as they grow taller.

'Imperial Giants'

RECOMMENDED

S. atropurpurea is an upright, branching plant growing up to 90 cm (36") tall and spreading about 30 cm (12"). Its flowers may be white, blue, purple or red. **'Imperial Giants'** plants bear blooms in a deep maroon colour as well as shades of pink.

S. stellata grows 45 cm (18") tall and spreads half as much. This plant bears small white flowers but is grown for its papery, orb-like seed-pods which dry in unusual globe shapes and are useful accents in dried arrangements. Pick *S. stellata* while still slightly green to keep the dried seedpods from shattering. **'Paper Moon'** ('Drumstick') bears blue flowers that dry to a warm bronze colour.

Snapdragon

Antirrhinum

Height: 15–120 cm (6–48") **Spread:** 15–60 cm (6–24")
Flower colour: white, cream, yellow, orange, red, maroon, pink, or bicoloured

*S*napdragons are one of the most appealing plants. The flower colours are always rich and vibrant, and even the most jaded gardeners are tempted to squeeze open the dragons' mouths. The plants vary from low, casual ramblers, at home in a rock garden or mixed planter, to tall, stately giants that can hold their own with heat-hating foxgloves and delphiniums.

PLANTING

Seeding: Indoors in late winter; direct sow in spring.

Planting out: After last frost.

Spacing: 15–45 cm (6–18"), depending on variety.

Snapdragons may self-sow, providing you with new plants each year.

GROWING

Snapdragons prefer **full sun** but will tolerate light or partial shade. The soil should be **fertile**, rich in **organic** matter and **well drained**. Snapdragons prefer a **neutral or alkaline** soil and will not perform as well in acidic soil. If sowing seeds on the soil surface, do not cover them because they require light for germination.

TIPS

The height of the variety dictates the best place for it in a border—the shortest varieties work well near the front, and the tallest look good in the centre or back of a border. The dwarf and medium-height varieties can also be used in planters, and there is even a variety available with a droopy habit that does well in a hanging basket.

The tallest of the snapdragons will probably need to be staked. To encourage bushier growth, pinch the tips of the plants while they are young.

Snapdragons are interesting and long lasting in fresh flower arrangements. The buds will continue to mature and open even after the spike is cut from the plant.

Cut off the flower spikes as they fade to promote further blooming and to prevent the plant from dying back before the end of the season. Snapdragons are perennials grown as annuals; they can tolerate cold nights well into fall but rarely survive winter. Self-sown seedlings may sprout the following spring if plants are left in place over winter.

RECOMMENDED

There are many cultivars of *A. majus* available. Snapdragons are grouped into three sizes: dwarf, medium and tall. The shortest, or dwarf, varieties grow up to 30 cm (12") tall. **'Floral Showers'** is a true dwarf, growing 15–20 cm (6–8") tall. This plant bears flowers in a wide range of solid and bicolours. **'Lampion'** is a new and interesting cultivar, usually grouped with the semi-dwarfs. It is a trailing plant that cascades up to 90 cm (36"). It is a great plant for hanging baskets. **'Princess'** bears white and purple bicoloured flowers. This plant produces many shoots from the base and therefore many flower spikes.

Medium-height snapdragons grow 30–60 cm (12–24") tall. **'Black Prince'** bears striking, dark purple-red flowers set against bronze-green foliage.

The tallest cultivars, or giants, can grow 90–120 cm (36–48") tall. **'Madam Butterfly'** is a tall cultivar that bears double flowers in a wide range of colours. The flowers of this cultivar don't 'snap,' as the hinged mouth structure is lost with the addition of the extra petals. **'Rocket'** series produces long spikes of brightly coloured flowers in many shades.

PROBLEMS & PESTS

Snapdragons can suffer from several fungal problems including powdery mildew, fungal leaf spot, root rot, wilt and downy mildew. Snapdragon rust is the worst. To prevent rust, avoid wetting the foliage when watering, choose rust-resistant varieties and plant snapdragons in different parts of the garden each year. Aphids are also sometimes a problem.

Spider Flower
Cleome
Cleome

Height: 90–180 cm (36–72") **Spread:** 45–90 cm (18–36")
Flower colour: pink, rose, violet or white

*T*all annuals are invaluable. Cleome adds height, movement and clear colours to the garden. As a bonus it often re-seeds. A lovely effect can be created by using Cleome, Cosmos and Nicotiana together. Cleome has tropical-looking foliage that adds an exotic touch to any garden.

The flowers can be cut for fresh arrangements, although the plants have an unusual odour that is very noticeable up close.

PLANTING

Seeding: Indoors in late winter; direct sow in spring.

Planting out: After last frost.

Spacing: 45–75 cm (18–30").

GROWING

Spider Flower prefers **full sun** but tolerates partial shade. Any kind of soil will do fine. Mix in plenty of **organic** matter to help the soil retain moisture. These plants are drought tolerant but will look and perform better if watered regularly. Don't water excessively or the plants will become leggy. Chill seeds overnight before planting.

'Royal Queen' series

Deadhead to prolong the blooming period and to minimize this plant's prolific self-sowing. Self-sown seedlings will start coming up almost as soon as the seeds hit the ground and can become invasive. Fortunately, the plants are very distinctive and can be quickly spotted poking up where they don't belong, making them easy to pull up while they are still young.

TIPS

Spider Flower can be planted in groups at the back of a border. This plant is also effective in the centre of an island bed; use lower-growing plants around the edges to hide the leafless lower stems of Spider Flower.

Be careful when handling these plants because they have nasty barbs along the stems.

RECOMMENDED

C. hasslerana is a tall, upright plant with strong, supple stems. The foliage and flowers of this plant have a strong, but not unpleasant, scent. **'Helen Campbell'** has white flowers. **'Royal Queen'** series has flowers in all colours, available by individual colour or as a mixture of all available colours. The varieties are named by their colour; e.g., **'Rose Queen,' 'Violet Queen'** and **'Cherry Queen.'** The varieties in this series are resistant to fading.

PROBLEMS & PESTS

Aphids may be a problem.

Statice
Limonium

Height: 30–60 cm (12–24") **Spread:** 15–30 cm (6–12")
Flower colour: blue, pink, white, yellow, orange, red or purple

*T*his is one of the best everlasting flowers to grow. In the garden Statice produces clouds of flowers in intriguing colours, some with jewel tones. The pale varieties look like patches of low-lying fog in the garden. Small groups of Statice randomly placed in a flowerbed create a nice contrast of form and flower with other plants.

PLANTING

Seeding: Indoors in mid-winter; direct sow in spring.

Planting out: After last frost.

Spacing: 15–30 cm (6–12").

GROWING

Statice prefers **full sun**. The soil should be of **poor or average fertility, light, sandy** and **well drained**. These plants don't like having their roots disturbed, so if starting them indoors, it is best to start them in peat pots. Germination takes 14–21 days.

TIPS

Statice makes an interesting addition to any sunny border, particularly in informal gardens. It is a perennial grown as an annual.

The basal leaves of Statice grow flat and in a circular motion similar to the habit of biennials. Because the stalk is sent up from the middle of the plant, the plants look better spaced more closely together than is usually recommended.

Cut Statice for drying late in summer, once the white centre has come out on the bloom. It's not necessary to hang Statice upside down to dry; simply stand the stalks in a vase with about one inch of water and they will dry quite nicely on their own.

RECOMMENDED

L. sinuatum forms a basal rosette of hairy leaves. Ridgy stems bear clusters of small papery flowers in blue, purple, pink or white. **'Fortress'** has strongly branching plants and flowers in several bright and pastel shades. The plants grow up to 60 cm (24") tall. **'Petite Bouquet'** series has compact, 30 cm (12") plants with flowers in blue, purple, pink,

white and yellow. **'Sunset'** grows 60 cm (24") tall and bears flowers in warm red, orange, yellow, apricot and salmon shades.

PROBLEMS & PESTS

Most problems can be avoided by providing a well-drained site and ensuring that there is good air circulation around the plants.

Statice is frequently grown in cutting gardens and can be used in fresh and dried arrangements.

Stock

Matthiola

Height: 20–90 cm (8–36") tall **Spread:** 30 cm (12")
Flower colour: pink, purple, red, rose or white.

*S*tocks have been greatly improved through hybridizing. Neat, erect plants produce dense, conical clusters of brightly coloured flowers. Night-scented Stock is unequalled for fragrance, but it can be a challenge to use because the plants look frazzled and wilted during the day. A good solution is to plant both Stock and Night-scented Stock and enjoy flowers by day and fragrance by night.

PLANTING

Seeding: Indoors in mid-winter; in mild climates, direct sow in fall.

Planting out: After last frost.

Spacing: 30 cm (12").

GROWING

Stock plants prefer **full sun** but will tolerate partial shade. The soil should be of **average fertility**, have lots of **organic** matter worked in and be **moist** but **well drained**. Start seeds indoors in mid-winter. Do not uncover seeds because they require light to germinate.

TIPS

Stocks can be used in mixed beds or in mass plantings. Night-scented Stock should be planted where its wonderful scent can be enjoyed in the evening—near windows that are left open, beside patios or along pathways.

It is best to place Night-scented Stock with other plants as these stocks tend to look wilted and bedraggled during the day, only to revive impressively at night.

RECOMMENDED

M. incana (Stock) has many cultivar groups with new ones introduced each year. Its colours range from pink and purple to red, rose or white. The height can be 20–90 cm (8–36"), depending on the cultivar. A popular cultivar is the **'Cinderella'** series. The compact plants in this series plants grow about 25 cm (10") tall and have fragrant, colourful flowers.

M. longipetala subsp. *bicornis* (Night-scented Stock; Evening-scented Stock) has pink or purple flowers that fill the evening air with their scent. The plants grow 30–45 cm (12–18") tall. **'Starlight Scentsation'** bears very fragrant flowers in a wide range of colours.

PROBLEMS & PESTS

Root rot or other fungal problems may occur. Slugs may be attracted to young foliage.

When cutting stock flowers for arrangements, cut and then crush the woody stems so they will draw water more easily.

Strawflower
Everlasting, Golden Everlasting
Bracteantha (Helichrysum)

Height: 30–150 cm (12–60") **Spread:** 30–60 cm (12–24")
Flower colour: yellow, red, orange, pink, white or purple

S trawflower has long been known for its attractive everlasting habit, but new varieties in pastel and bright colours are fresh additions to the garden. The daisy-like flowers bloom for a very long time, everlasting in the garden as well as in dried arrangements.

PLANTING

Seeding: Indoors in early spring; direct sow after last frost.

Planting out: After last frost.

Spacing: 25–45 cm (10–18").

GROWING

Strawflower prefers to be planted in locations that receive **full sun**. The soil should be of **average fertility, sandy, moist** and **well drained**. Strawflower is drought tolerant.

When sowing seeds in the garden, do not cover them because they require light to germinate.

TIPS

Include Strawflower in mixed beds, borders and containers. The lowest-growing varieties are useful edging plants. Taller varieties may require staking.

RECOMMENDED

B. bracteata (*H. bracteatum*) is a tall, upright plant with grey-green foliage that bears brightly coloured papery flowers. The species can grow up to 150 cm (60") tall, but the cultivars are generally a bit more compact. **'Bright Bikini'** series has large, colourful flowers on compact plants that grow to about 30 cm (12") tall. **'Pastel'** mixed has smaller flowers in soft tones that blend in well with other colours.

PROBLEMS & PESTS

Strawflower is susceptible to downy mildew.

The most popular use of Strawflower is for fresh or dried flower arrangements. To dry, hang fully opened flowers upside down in bunches.

Sunflower
Helianthus

Height: dwarf varieties, 60 cm (24"); giants up to 4.5 m (15')
Spread: 30–60 cm (12–24") **Flower colour:** most commonly yellow but also orange, red, brown or cream; typically with brown, purple or rusty-red centres.

*I*n the grip of a long winter, how we long to see the mesmerizing fields of yellow-gold sunflowers of August and September. In our own gardens the colour range is exciting. 'Prado Red' is a velvety mahogany; 'Valentine' is a creamy yellow. At the back of the border they are an imposing presence, and dwarf sunflowers such as 'Teddy Bear' and 'Music Box' can be mixed through the middle of the border.

PLANTING
Seeding: Indoors in late winter; direct sow in spring.

Planting out: After last frost.

Spacing: 30–60 cm (12–24").

GROWING

Sunflowers grow best in **full sun**. The soil should be of **average fertility, humus rich, moist** and **well drained**.

Sunflowers are excellent plants for children to grow. The seeds are big and easy to handle, and they germinate quickly. The plants grow continually upwards, and their progress can be measured until the flower finally appears on top of the tall plant. If planted along the wall of a two-storey house, the progress can be observed from above as well as below, and the flowers are easy to see.

TIPS

The lower-growing varieties can be used in beds and borders. The tall varieties are effective at the backs of borders and make good screens and temporary hedges. The tallest varieties will need staking.

Birds will flock to the ripening seedheads of your sunflowers, quickly plucking clean the tightly

Sunflowers are grown as a crop seed for roasting, snacking, baking or for producing oil or flour. Use grey-seeded varieties for eating.

'Valentine'

packed seeds. If you plan to keep the seeds to eat, you will have to place a mesh net, the sort used to keep birds out of cherry trees, around the flower-heads until the seeds ripen. This can be a bit of a nuisance and doesn't look too nice; most gardeners leave the flowers to the birds and buy seeds for personal eating.

RECOMMENDED

H. annuus (Common Sunflower) is considered weedy, but the development of many new cultivars has revived the use of this plant. **'Music Box'**

'Teddy Bear' (above), 'Prado Red' (below)

grows about 75 cm (30") tall and has flowers in all colours, including some bicolours. **'Prado Red'** bears deep mahagony flowers and grows up to 1.5 m (5'). **'Russian Giant'** grows up to 3 m (10') tall and bears yellow flowers and large seeds. **'Teddy Bear'** has fuzzy-looking double flowers on compact plants 60–90 cm (24–36") tall. **'Valentine'** bears creamy-yellow flowers and grows up to 1.5 m (5').

PROBLEMS & PESTS

Powdery mildew may affect these plants.

'Teddy Bear'

Swan River Daisy

Brachycome

Height: 20–45 cm (8–18") **Spread:** equal to or slightly greater than height
Flower colour: blue or pink (usually tinged purple); white with yellow centres

Swan River Daisy is superb in containers or flower beds. The plants produce a lot of flowers in pale to deep tones of lilac, blue, purple and white. These daisies are good companions for salvias, Heliotrope and grey-leaved plants such as Dusty Miller and the perennial Artemisia.

PLANTING
Seeding: Indoors in late winter; direct-sow in mid-spring.

Planting out: Early spring.

Spacing: 30 cm (12").

GROWING
Swan River Daisy prefers **full sun** but can benefit from light shade in the afternoon to prevent the plant from over-heating. The soil should be **fertile** and **well drained**. Allow the soil to dry between waterings.

Plant out early because cool spring weather encourages compact, sturdy growth. This plant is frost tolerant and tends to die back when the summer gets too hot. Cut it back if it begins to fade, and don't plant it in hot areas of the garden.

TIPS
These versatile plants are useful for edging beds and work well in rock gardens, mixed containers and hanging baskets.

Plant Swan River Daisy with plants that take longer to grow in. As Swan River Daisy is fading in July, the companions will be filling in and beginning to flower.

RECOMMENDED
B. iberidifolia forms a bushy, spreading mound of feathery foliage. Blue-purple or pink-purple daisy-like flowers are borne all summer. **'Bravo'** bears flowers in white, blue, purple or pink and flowers profusely in a cool but bright spot in the garden. **'Splendor'** series has dark-centered flowers in pink, purple or white.

PROBLEMS & PESTS
Occasionally aphids, slugs or snails will cause some trouble for this plant.

The flowers are fragrant and long lasting when cut for arrangements.

Sweet Alyssum

Lobularia

Height: 8–30 cm (3–12") **Spread:** 15–60 cm (6–24")
Flower colour: pink, purple or white

Gardeners have barely taken their winter gloves off when Sweet Alyssum starts appearing in nurseries. It is commonplace, but it has many worthwhile qualities. It re-seeds, it is scented, and in autumn it revives, becoming fresh and fragrant again. It pops up along pathways and between stones, giving summer a sweet sendoff.

PLANTING

Seeding: Indoors in late winter; direct sow in spring.

Planting out: Once soil has warmed.

Spacing: 20–30 cm (8–12").

GROWING

Sweet Alyssum prefers **full sun** but will tolerate light shade. Soil with **average fertility** is preferred but poor soil is tolerated. The soil should be **well drained**. These plants dislike having their roots disturbed, so if starting them indoors, use peat pots or pellets. Trim Sweet Alyssum back occasionally over summer to keep it flowering and looking good.

'Wonderland' series

TIPS

Sweet Alyssum will creep around rock gardens, on rock walls, between paving stones and along the edges of beds. It is also good for filling in the spaces between taller plants in borders and mixed containers.

Leave Sweet Alyssum out all winter. In spring, remove the previous year's plant to expose self-sown seedlings below.

RECOMMENDED

L. maritima forms a low, spreading mound of foliage. The entire plant appears to be covered in tiny blossoms when it is in full flower. **'Pastel Carpet'** bears flowers in rose, white, violet and mauve. **'Snow Crystal'** bears large, bright, white flowers profusely all summer. **'Wonderland'** series offers a mix of all colours on compact plants.

PROBLEMS & PESTS

Sweet Alyssum rarely has any problems but is sometimes afflicted with downy mildew.

The 'Sweet' in the name is a reference to the plant's lovely fragrant flowers.

Sweet Pea

Lathyrus

Height: 30–180 cm (12–72") **Spread:** 15–30 cm (6–12")
Flower colour: pink, red, purple, lavender, blue, salmon, pale yellow, peach, white or bicoloured

S weet Peas are one of the most enchanting annuals, but I seldom see them grown. One of the few times I saw a robust planting was at the Georgian Bay cottage of Harold Ballard, who was the owner of the Toronto Maple Leafs. Climbing the chainlink fence surrounding his property was the most lush planting of Sweet Peas I had ever seen. He loved them, as do thousands of other gardeners. Their fragrance is intoxicating, and the flowers in double tones and shimmering shades look like no other annual in the garden.

PLANTING

Seeding: Direct sow in early spring.

Spacing: 15–30 cm (6–12").

GROWING

Sweet Peas prefer **full sun** but tolerate light shade. The soil should be **fertile,** high in **organic** matter, **moist** and **well drained**. The plants will tolerate light frost.

Soak seeds in water for 24 hours or nick them with a nail file before planting them. Planting a second crop of Sweet Peas about a month after the first one will ensure a longer blooming period. Deadhead all spent blooms.

TIPS

Sweet Peas will grow up poles, trellises, fences or over rocks. The low-growing varieties will form low, shrubby mounds. An excellent way to provide privacy and hide a chain-link fence is to grow Sweet Peas up it.

To help prevent some diseases from afflicting your Sweet Peas, avoid planting Sweet Peas in the same location two years in a row.

Fertilize very lightly during the flowering season.

RECOMMENDED

There are many cultivars of **L. odoratus** available. **'Bijou'** series is a popular heat-resistant variety that grows 45 cm (18") tall, with an equal spread. It needs no support to grow. **'Bouquet'** mixed is a tall, climbing variety. **'Supersnoop'** series is a sturdy bush type that needs no support. The plant is fragrant with long stems. Pinch its tips to encourage low growth.

PROBLEMS & PESTS

Slugs and snails may eat the foliage of young plants. Root rot, mildew, rust and leaf spot may also afflict Sweet Peas occasionally.

Sweet Peas are attractive and long lasting as cut flowers. Cutting Sweet Pea flowers encourages more blooms.

Verbena
Garden Verbena
Verbena

Height: 20–180 cm (8–72") **Spread:** 30–60 cm (12–24")
Flower colour: red, pink, purple, blue or white; usually with white centres

One of the most reward-ing verbenas to have in the garden is *V. bonar-iensis.* The purple flowers of this plant bloom on stiff, wiry stems about 1.5 m (5') tall. Because the blooms are held so high, it is easy to see through the foliage at the bottom to the plantings behind. Verbenas are also attractive in the middle of a border where the flowers could rise above other annuals such as Nicotiana or Cosmos. The low, spreading hybrid verbenas make an excellent addition to mixed container plantings and the front of mixed borders.

PLANTING

Seeding: Indoors in mid-winter.

Planting out: After last frost.

Spacing: 45 cm (18") apart.

For fall blooms, cut back the plants to half their size in mid-summer.

GROWING

Verbenas grow best in **full sun**. The soil should be **fertile** and **very well drained**.

Chill seeds one week before sowing. Moisten the soil before sowing seeds. Do not cover the seeds with soil. Place the entire seed tray or pots in darkness. Water only if the soil becomes very dry. Once the seeds germinate, they can be moved into the light.

TIPS

Use verbenas on rock walls, in beds, borders, rock gardens, containers, hanging baskets and window boxes. They are good substitutes for ivy geraniums where the sun is hot and where a roof overhang keeps these mildew-prone plants dry.

Pinch back young plants for bushy growth.

RECOMMENDED

V. bonariensis forms a low clump of foliage from which tall, stiff, flower-bearing stems emerge. The small purple flowers are held in clusters. This plant grows up to 180 cm (72") tall, but spreads only 45–60 cm (18–24"). It may self-seed, and this species may survive a mild winter in southern Ontario.

V. x hybrida is a bushy plant that may be upright or spreading. It bears clusters of small flowers in shades of white, purple, blue, pink, red or yellow. **'Peaches and Cream'** is a spreading plant with flowers that open to a soft peach colour and

fade to white. **'Romance'** series has red, pink, purple or white flowers, with white eyes. The plants grow to 20–25 cm (8–10") tall. **'Showtime'** bears brightly coloured flowers on compact plants that grow to 25 cm (10") tall and spread 45 cm (18").

PROBLEMS & PESTS

Aphids, whiteflies, slugs and snails may be troublesome. Avoid fungal problems by making sure there is good air circulation around the plant.

'Romance' series

Viola

Viola

Height: 8–25 cm (3–10") **Spread:** 15–30 cm (6–12")
Flower colour: blue, purple, red, orange, yellow, pink, white or multi-coloured

*V*iolas have amusing and charming little faces on flowers in the colours of the rainbow. Many of the flowers have lines like little cat's whiskers, and bloom in two tones. They are so welcome in the spring garden. Use them as graceful underpinnings to plantings of stiff-stemmed bulbs. They will nap during the hottest part of summer, but revive in cool weather.

PLANTING

Seeding: Indoors in early winter or mid-summer.

Planting out: Early spring or early fall.

Spacing: 15 cm (6").

Johnny-jump-up gets its name from the fact that it re-seeds profusely and tends to show up in the most unlikely places. This small plant has an affinity for lawns and just about any nook or cranny it can find to grow in.

GROWING

Violas prefer **full sun** but will tolerate partial shade. The soil should be **fertile, moist** and **well drained.**

Direct sowing is not recommended. Sow seeds indoors in early winter for spring flowers and in midsummer for fall and early-winter blooms. Germination will be greater if seeds are kept in darkness until they germinate. Place seed trays in a dark closet or cover with dark plastic or layers of newspaper to provide enough darkness.

Violas do well when the weather is cool. They may even die back completely in summer. Plants may rejuvenate in fall, but it is often easier to plant new ones in fall and not take up summer garden space with plants that don't look good.

V. × wittrockiana

TIPS

Violas can be used in beds and borders, and they are popular for mixing in with spring-flowering bulbs. They can also be grown in containers. The large-flowering violas are preferred for early-spring colour among primroses in garden beds.

V. × wittrockiana

RECOMMENDED

V. tricolor (Johnny-jump-up) is a popular species. The flowers are purple, white and yellow, usually in combination, although several varieties have flowers in a single colour, often purple. This plant will thrive in gravel. **'Bowles Black'** has dark purple flowers that appear to be almost black. The centre of each flower is yellow. **'Helen Mound'** ('Helen Mount') bears large flowers in the traditional purple, yellow and white combination.

V. x wittrockiana (Pansy) comes in blue, purple, red, orange, yellow, pink and white, often multi-coloured or with face-like markings. **'Floral Dance'** is popular for spring and fall displays as it is quite cold hardy; it has flowers in a variety of solid colours and multi-colours. **'Imperial'** series

V. tricolor (above), *V. × wittrockiana* (below)

bears large flowers in a good range of unique colours. For example, **'Imperial Frosty Rose'** has flowers with deep rose pink centres that gradually pale to white near the edges of the petals. **'Joker'** series has bicoloured or multi-coloured flowers with distinctive face markings. The flowers come in all colours. **'Maxim Marina'** bears light blue flowers with white-rimmed dark blue blotches at the centre. This cultivar is tolerant of both hot and cold temperatures. **'Watercolor'** series is a newer group of cultivars with flowers in delicate pastel shades.

PROBLEMS & PESTS

Slugs and snails can be problems. There are also some fungal problems that can be avoided through good air circulation and good drainage.

Collect short vases, such as perfume bottles with narrow necks, for displaying the cut flowers of pansies and violets. The more you pick, the more profusely the plants will bloom. These flowers are also among the easiest to press between sheets of wax paper, weighted down with stacks of books.

Zinnia

Zinnia

Height: 15–90 cm (6–36"), depending on variety **Spread:** 30 cm (12")
Flower colour: red, yellow, green, purple, orange, pink or white

Zinnias bloom in sizzling colours that perk up the most jaded gardeners. What other flower can combine hot pink and orange as successfully as a zinnia? The combination of eye-popping colour and strong structure gives zinnias a pleasing profile in the garden. These flowers are bold but never garish.

PLANTING

Seeding: Indoors in late winter; direct sow after last frost.

Planting out: After last frost.

Spacing: 15–30 cm (6–12").

GROWING

Zinnias grow best in **full sun**. The soil should be **fertile,** rich in **organic** matter, **moist** and **well drained.** When starting the seeds indoors, plant them in individual peat pots to avoid disturbing the roots when transplanting.

Zinnias make excellent, long-lasting cut flowers for fresh arrangements.

TIPS

Zinnias are useful in beds and borders, in containers and in cutting gardens. The dwarf varieties can be used as edging plants. They are great for fall colour. Combine the rounded form of the zinnia flower with the spiky blooms of sun-loving salvia, or use the taller varieties in front of sunflowers in fertile soil in a dry, sunny location both plants will love.

Deadhead zinnias to keep them flowering and looking their best. To keep mildew from the leaves, plant mildew-resistant varieties and avoid wetting the foliage when you water.

RECOMMENDED

Z. elegans flowers come in several forms including single, double and cactus flowered. On a cactus-flowered bloom, the petals appear to be rolled into

Cactus-flowered zinnia (above), 'Profusion White' (below)

tubes like the spines of a cactus. **'California Giants'** are bushy plants growing to 90 cm (36") and bearing large double flowers in a wide range of colours. **'Peter Pan'** grows up to 30 cm (12") tall, but it starts blooming early at 15 cm (6"), with flowers in mixed colours. **'Thumbelina'** series has small flowers in all colours on dwarf, 15 cm (6"), weather-resistant plants.

Z. **'Profusion'** is a fast-growing, mildew-resistant hybrid. It has flowers in bright, orange or cherry red on compact plants that grow 25–30 cm (10–12") tall.

PROBLEMS & PESTS

Zinnias are prone to mildew and other fungal problems. Prevent such problems by ensuring good air circulation and drainage for the plants.

Though zinnias are quite drought tolerant, they will grow best if watered thoroughly when the soil dries out. Use a soaker hose to avoid wetting the leaves.

Quick Reference Chart
HEIGHT LEGEND: Low: < 30 cm (12") • Medium: 30–60 cm (12–24") • Tall: > 60 cm (24")

SPECIES by Common Name	COLOUR									SOWING		HEIGHT		
	White	Pink	Red	Orange	Yellow	Blue	Purple	Green	Foliage	Indoors	Direct	Low	Medium	Tall
African Daisy	*	*	*	*	*					*	*		*	
Ageratum	*	*				*	*			*	*	*	*	
Amaranth			*		*			*	*	*	*			*
Angel's Trumpet	*				*		*			*				*
Baby's Breath	*	*					*			*	*		*	*
Bachelor's Buttons	*	*	*			*	*			*	*		*	*
Bacopa	*						*					*		
Begonia	*	*	*	*	*				*	*		*	*	
Bells-of-Ireland								*		*	*			*
Black-eyed Susan			*	*	*					*	*	*	*	*
Black-eyed Susan Vine	*			*	*					*	*			*
Blanket Flower			*	*	*					*	*		*	*
Blue Lace Flower	*					*	*			*	*		*	
Blue Marguerite	*					*				*	*	*	*	
Browallia	*					*	*			*		*	*	
Calendula	*			*	*					*	*	*	*	
California Poppy	*	*	*	*	*		*				*	*	*	
Candytuft	*	*	*				*			*	*	*		
Canterbury Bells	*	*				*	*			*			*	*
Cape Marigold	*	*		*	*					*	*		*	
Chilean Glory Flower			*	*						*				*
China Aster	*	*	*	*	*	*	*			*	*	*	*	*
Chinese Forget-me-not	*	*				*				*	*		*	
Chrysanthemum	*		*		*		*				*		*	*
Cockscomb		*	*	*	*		*			*	*	*	*	*
Coleus							*		*	*		*	*	*
Coreopsis			*	*	*		*			*	*	*	*	*
Cosmos	*	*	*	*	*		*			*	*		*	*

Quick Reference Chart

HARDINESS			LIGHT				SOIL CONDITIONS						Page Number	SPECIES by Common Name
Hardy	Half-hardy	Tender	Sun	Part Shade	Light Shade	Shade	Moist	Well Drained	Dry	Fertile	Average	Poor		
		*	*				*	*	*		*		46	African Daisy
		*	*	*	*		*	*		*			48	Ageratum
		*	*					*			*	*	52	Amaranth
		*	*				*	*		*			56	Angel's Trumpet
*			*					*	*			*	60	Baby's Breath
*			*				*	*	*	*	*	*	62	Bachelor's Buttons
		*	*	*			*	*			*		64	Bacopa
		*		*	*			*		*			66	Begonia
	*		*	*			*	*			*		70	Bells-of-Ireland
	*		*	*			*	*			*		72	Black-eyed Susan
		*	*	*	*		*	*		*			76	Black-eyed Susan Vine
*			*					*	*		*	*	78	Blanket Flower
*			*					*			*		80	Blue Lace Flower
	*		*					*			*		82	Blue Marguerite
		*	*	*	*	*		*		*			84	Browallia
*			*	*				*			*		86	Calendula
*			*					*	*		*	*	88	California Poppy
*			*					*			*	*	92	Candytuft
*			*	*			*			*			94	Canterbury Bells
	*		*					*	*	*			96	Cape Marigold
	*		*					*		*			98	Chilean Glory Flower
	*		*	*			*			*			100	China Aster
*			*	*			*	*			*		102	Chinese Forget-me-not
*	*		*	*				*			*		104	Chrysanthemum
		*	*				*	*		*			106	Cockscomb
		*		*	*		*	*		*	*		110	Coleus
*			*					*	*	*	*		114	Coreopsis
		*	*					*	*		*	*	116	Cosmos

Quick Reference Chart

HEIGHT LEGEND: Low: < 30 cm (12") • Medium: 30–60 cm (12–24") • Tall: > 60 cm (24")

SPECIES by Common Name	COLOUR									SOWING		HEIGHT		
	White	Pink	Red	Orange	Yellow	Blue	Purple	Green	Foliage	Indoors	Direct	Low	Medium	Tall
Creeping Zinnia				*	*						*	*		
Cup Flower	*					*	*			*		*		
Cup-and-saucer Vine	*						*			*				*
Dahlberg Daisy				*	*					*	*	*		
Dahlia	*	*	*	*	*		*					*	*	*
Diascia		*								*		*		
Dusty Miller	*				*				*	*			*	
Dwarf Morning Glory		*				*	*			*	*	*	*	
Fan Flower						*	*			*		*		
Forget-me-not	*	*				*				*	*	*		
Four-o'clock Flower	*	*	*		*					*	*		*	*
Fuchsia	*	*	*				*					*	*	*
Ganzania	*	*	*	*	*					*	*	*	*	
Geranium	*	*	*	*		*	*			*	*	*	*	
Globe Amaranth	*	*	*				*			*		*	*	*
Godetia	*	*	*				*				*		*	*
Heliotrope	*						*			*		*	*	
Hollyhock	*	*	*		*		*			*				*
Impatiens	*	*	*	*			*		*	*		*	*	*
Licorice Plant	*				*				*				*	
Livingstone Daisy	*	*	*	*	*					*	*	*		
Lobelia	*	*	*			*	*			*		*		
Love-in-a-mist	*	*				*	*			*	*		*	
Madagascar Periwinkle	*	*	*				*			*		*	*	
Mallow	*	*								*	*		*	*
Marigold	*		*	*	*					*		*	*	*
Mexican Sunflower			*	*	*					*	*			*
Million Bells	*	*		*	*		*					*		

Quick Reference Chart

Hardy	Half-hardy	Tender	Sun	Part Shade	Light Shade	Shade	Moist	Well Drained	Dry	Fertile	Average	Poor	Page Number	SPECIES by Common Name
		*	*					*			*		120	Creeping Zinnia
	*		*	*			*			*			122	Cup Flower
		*	*					*			*		124	Cup-and-saucer Vine
*			*					*			*	*	126	Dahlberg Daisy
		*	*				*	*		*			128	Dahlia
	*			*	*		*			*			132	Diascia
	*		*		*			*			*		134	Dusty Miller
		*	*					*			*	*	136	Dwarf Morning Glory
		*	*		*		*	*			*		138	Fan Flower
*				*	*		*			*			140	Forget-me-not
		*	*	*				*		*	*	*	142	Four-o'clock Flower
		*		*	*		*	*		*			144	Fuchsia
		*	*	*				*			*	*	148	Gazania
		*	*	*				*		*			150	Geranium
		*	*					*			*		154	Globe Amaranth
*			*		*		*	*			*	*	156	Godetia
		*	*				*			*			158	Heliotrope
*			*	*				*			*	*	162	Hollyhock
		*		*	*	*	*	*		*			166	Impatiens
	*		*				*	*			*	*	170	Licorice Plant
		*	*					*			*	*	172	Livingstone Daisy
*			*	*	*		*			*			174	Lobelia
*			*					*			*		176	Love-in-a-mist
		*	*	*			*	*	*	*	*	*	178	Madagascar Periwinkle
*			*				*	*	*		*		180	Mallow
	*		*					*			*		184	Marigold
		*	*					*	*		*	*	188	Mexican Sunflower
	*		*				*	*		*			190	Million Bells

Quick Reference Chart
HEIGHT LEGEND: Low: < 30 cm (12") • Medium: 30–60 cm (12–24") • Tall: > 60 cm (24")

SPECIES by Common Name	White	Pink	Red	Orange	Yellow	Blue	Purple	Green	Foliage	Indoors	Direct	Low	Medium	Tall
Monkey Flower	*	*	*	*	*		*			*		*		
Morning Glory	*	*				*	*			*	*			*
Nasturtium	*	*	*	*	*				*	*	*	*		*
Nicotiana	*	*	*		*		*	*		*	*	*	*	*
Painted-tongue		*	*	*	*		*			*	*		*	
Passion Flower	*	*				*	*							*
Petunia	*	*	*		*		*			*		*	*	
Phlox	*	*	*		*	*	*				*	*	*	
Poppy	*	*	*	*	*		*				*			*
Portulaca	*	*	*	*	*		*			*		*		
Prairie Gentian	*	*			*	*	*			*		*	*	
Rocket Larkspur	*	*				*	*			*	*		*	*
Salvia	*	*	*	*		*	*			*	*	*	*	*
Scabiosa	*	*				*	*			*	*		*	*
Snapdragon	*	*	*	*	*		*			*	*	*	*	*
Spider Flower	*	*					*			*	*			*
Statice	*	*	*	*	*	*	*			*	*		*	
Stock	*	*	*				*			*		*	*	*
Strawflower	*	*	*	*	*		*			*	*		*	*
Sunflower	*		*	*	*					*	*		*	*
Swan River Daisy		*				*	*			*	*	*	*	
Sweet Alyssum	*	*					*			*	*	*		
Sweet Pea	*	*	*		*	*	*				*	*		*
Verbena	*	*	*			*	*			*		*	*	*
Viola	*	*	*	*	*	*	*			*		*		
Zinnia	*	*	*	*	*		*	*		*	*	*	*	*

Quick Reference Chart

Hardy	Half-hardy	Tender	Sun	Part Shade	Light Shade	Shade	Moist	Well Drained	Dry	Fertile	Average	Poor	Page Number	SPECIES by Common Name
	*	*		*	*		*			*			192	Monkey Flower
		*	*					*			*	*	194	Morning Glory
		*	*	*			*	*			*	*	198	Nasturtium
		*	*	*	*		*			*			202	Nicotiana
		*	*					*		*			206	Painted-tongue
*			*	*			*	*		*			208	Passion Flower
	*		*					*			*	*	210	Petunia
*			*				*			*			214	Phlox
*			*					*		*			216	Poppy
		*	*					*	*			*	220	Portulaca
	*		*	*	*			*			*		224	Prairie Gentian
*			*		*			*		*			226	Rocket Larkspur
	*	*	*		*		*	*		*	*		230	Salvia
	*		*					*		*	*		234	Scabiosa
	*		*	*	*		*	*		*			236	Snapdragon
	*		*	*			*		*	*	*	*	240	Spider Flower
		*	*					*	*		*	*	244	Statice
*			*	*			*	*		*			246	Stock
	*		*				*	*	*	*			248	Strawflower
*			*				*	*		*			250	Sunflower
	*		*	*				*	*	*			254	Swan River Daisy
*			*		*			*			*	*	256	Sweet Alyssum
*			*		*		*			*			258	Sweet Pea
*		*	*					*	*	*			260	Verbena
*			*	*			*			*			262	Viola
		*	*				*	*		*			266	Zinnia

GLOSSARY

Acid soil: soil with a pH lower than 7.0

Alkaline soil: soil with a pH higher than 7.0

Annual: a plant that germinates, flowers, sets seed and dies in one growing season

Basal leaves: leaves that form from the crown

Biennial: a plant that germinates and produces stems, roots and leaves in the first growing season; it flowers, sets seed and dies in the second growing season

Crown: the part of a plant at or just below soil level where the shoots join the roots

Cultivar: a cultivated plant variety with one or more distinct differences from the species, such as flower colour, leaf variegation or disease resistance

Damping off: fungal disease causing seedlings to rot at soil level and topple over

Deadhead: to remove spent flowers to maintain a neat appearance and encourage a longer blooming period

Disbud: to remove some flowerbuds to improve the size or quality of the remaining ones

Dormancy: a period of plant inactivity, usually during winter or unfavourable climatic conditions

Double flower: a flower with an unusually large number of petals, often caused by mutation of the stamens into petals

Genus: a category of biological classification between the species and family levels; the first word in a Latin name indicates the genus

Half-hardy: a plant capable of surviving the climatic conditions of a given region if protected

Harden off: to gradually acclimatize plants that have been growing in a protective environment to a more harsh environment, e.g., plants started indoors being moved outdoors

Hardy: capable of surviving unfavourable conditions, such as cold weather

Humus: decomposed or decomposing organic material in the soil

Hybrid: a plant resulting from natural or human-induced cross-breeding between varieties, species, or genera; the hybrid expresses features of each parent plant

Neutral soil: soil with a pH of 7.0

Node: the area on a stem from which a leaf or new shoot grows

pH: a measure of acidity or alkalinity (the lower the pH, the higher the acidity); the pH of soil influences availability of nutrients for plants

Perennial: a plant that takes three or more years to complete its life cycle; a herbaceous perennial normally dies back to the ground over winter

Rhizome: a food-storing stem that grows horizontally at or just below soil level, from which new shoots may emerge

Rootball: the root mass and surrounding soil of a container-grown plant or a plant dug out of the ground

Semi-double flower: a flower with petals that form two or three rings

Single flower: a flower with a single ring of typically four or five petals

Species: the original species from which cultivars and varieties are derived; the fundamental unit of biological classification

Subspecies (subsp.): a naturally occurring, regional form of a species, often isolated from other subspecies but still potentially interfertile with them

Taproot: a root system consisting of one main root with smaller roots branching from it

Tender: incapable of surviving the climatic conditions of a given region and requiring protection from frost or cold

True: describes the passing of desirable characteristics from the parent plant to seed-grown offspring; also called breeding true to type

Tuber: the thick section of a rhizome bearing nodes and buds

Variegation: foliage that has more than one colour, often patched or striped or bearing differently coloured leaf margins

Variety (var.): a naturally occurring variant of a species; below the level of subspecies in biological classification

INDEX